The Revolt of 1916 in Russian Central Asia

The Revolt of 1916 in Russian Central Asia

Edward Dennis Sokol

With a Foreword by S. Frederick Starr

JOHNS HOPKINS UNIVERSITY PRESS   BALTIMORE

Printed in the United States of America on acid-free paper
9 8 7 6 5 4 3 2 1

Johns Hopkins University Press
2715 North Charles Street
Baltimore, Maryland 21218-4363
www.press.jhu.edu

Library of Congress Cataloging-in-Publication Data

Names: Sokol, Edward D., author.
Title: The revolt of 1916 in Russian Central Asia / Edward Dennis Sokol ; with a foreword by S. Frederick Starr.
Description: Baltimore, Maryland : Johns Hopkins University Press, 2016. | Originally published: 1954. | Includes bibliographical references and index.
Identifiers: LCCN 2015043854| ISBN 9781421420509 (pbk. : alk. paper) | ISBN 9781421420516 (electronic) | ISBN 1421420503 (pbk. : alk. paper) | ISBN 1421420511 (electronic)
Subjects: LCSH: Asia, Central—History—Revolt, 1916. | World War, 1914–1918—Asia, Central. | Genocide—Asia, Central—History—20th century.
Classification: LCC DK858 .S65 2016 | DDC 958.43/083—dc23 LC record available at http://lccn.loc.gov/2015043854

A catalog record for this book is available from the British Library.

Johns Hopkins University Press uses environmentally friendly book materials, including recycled text paper that is composed of at least 30 percent post-consumer waste, whenever possible.

Contents

Foreword, by S. Frederick Starr vii

Preface xi

1 The Revolt of 1916 1

2 The Economic Background to the Revolt of 1916 11

A. Russian Economic Interests in Central Asia before the Conquest 11

B. Russian Economic Policy towards the Sarts 15

1. Land Policy 15
2. The Introduction of American Cotton 16
3. The Russians in Turkistan 22

C. Russian Economic Policy towards the Nomads 24

3 The Political Background to the Revolt of 1916 37

A. The Administration of the Country 37

B. The Political Situation up to 1898 46

C. The Andijan Uprising 50

D. The Political Situation after 1898 59

1. Enquiry of Count Palen 59
2. The Political Situation among the Sarts 59
3. The Political Situation among the Kazakhs and Kirghiz 63

4 The Revolt of 1916: First Phase 67

A. War Comes to Turkistan 67

B. The Reaction of the Natives to the War 69

C. The Supreme Command of June 25 73

D. Meeting of the Governors of the Central Asian Krai 74

E. The Revolt among the Sarts 78

F. The Appointment of General Kuropatkin as Governor-General 93

5 The Revolt of 1916: Second Phase 95
A. The Revolt of the Kirghiz and Kazakhs 95
1. The Announcement of the Supreme Order 95
2. The Revolt in the Steppe Oblasts 102
3. The Revolt in Semipalatinsk 108
4. The Revolt in Semirechie 111
5. The Flight of the Insurgents to China 127
B. The Revolt of the Turkomans 135

6 The End of the Revolt 139
A. Group Participation in the Revolt of 1916 139
1. The Well-to-Do Groups 139
2. The Poor 143
B. The Question of Foreign Influence 145
C. Measures Taken for the Securing of Peace in the Future 151
1. Military Measures 151
2. Administrative Measures 154
D. The Balance Sheet of Damage Suffered 155
E. The Dispatch of Workers to the Front 159
F. The Duma and the Revolt 163

7 The Revolt in Retrospect 165
A. The Early Soviet Interpretation of the Revolt 165
B. The Recent Soviet Interpretation 170
C. In Summing Up 175

Bibliography 181

Index 185

Foreword

A century ago approximately 270,000 Central Asians—Kazakhs, Tajiks, Turkmen, Uzbeks, and especially Kyrgyz—perished in one of the most ghastly mass deaths in modern history. This horrific killing took place when Russian officials attempted to draft natives of the region to fight and provide labor service for the tsar during World War I. In addition to those killed outright, tens of thousands more died while trying to escape over treacherous mountain passes into neighboring Xinjiang, China. Even today, bones of victims of this disaster continue to wash out from the rocky bottoms of deep crevasses in the Tian Shan mountains.

The scale of this demographic disaster is hard to grasp. Recent experts calculate that the Kyrgyz, who suffered most heavily, lost fully 40% of their total population.[1] All age groups suffered, but younger males died in disproportionate numbers, causing a demographic breakdown that is still felt today. It is estimated that had the tragedy of 1916 not occurred, the population of the Kyrgyz Republic would be twice what it is today.

Unlike the Armenian genocide, which was unfolding in Turkey at almost the same time, this mass killing of more than a quarter million people has been largely expunged from the world's historical consciousness. There are good reasons for this. Even as the last phase of the 1916 Uprising was taking place in Turkmenistan, Lenin and his Bolsheviks were overthrowing the tsarist government in St. Petersburg and establishing Soviet rule. During the first years after the Bolshevik coup, informative articles on the events of 1916 appeared in Russia, but by the end of the 1920s these ceased. As Lenin's heirs strove to establish

1. *Vosstanie 1916 goda: Documenty i materialy*, ed. K. Mambetaliev (Bishkek, 2015), pp. 248–249.

the Soviet Union as a multinational empire, the tragic events of 1916 became a taboo subject. They disappeared from the history books, and the Central Asians themselves were forbidden to delve into them. With the exception of a couple of minor studies from the 1960s, the scholarly literature on the 1916 Uprising dates mainly from the 1990s, after the collapse of the USSR. But even today the Putin government bans access to the tsarist archives in Moscow, where records of the events leading up to 1916 and of the Uprising itself are housed.

The one exception to this general silence, and a very worthy one, appeared in 1954, when an enterprising young American scholar, Edward Dennis Sokol of Johns Hopkins University, published the short book that is here reissued. Sokol modestly considered his study to be "a pioneering work rather than a definitive study," but his accomplishment was impressive by any standard. He exhaustively researched all published sources available at the time, and especially the documents and articles that were issued in such early Soviet periodicals as *Krasnyi Arkhiv* (*The Red Archive*). Moreover, he presented his findings in a calm and dispassionate manner that allows readers to draw their own conclusions.

The very structure of Sokol's book reflects his realization that the 1916 Uprising was about more than the drafting of young Kyrgyz and other Central Asians to fight with the tsarist army in World War I or to staff Russia's arms factories. By devoting nearly half of his study to the specific policies of Russian rule in Central Asia he implies that 1916 marked the culmination of several generations of steady Russian encroachment against the land and rights of the indigenous peoples and the product of the utter corruption that permeated Russian rule there. The 1916 Uprising, then, was a revolt against Russian colonialism in all its dimensions—economic, political, religious, and national—and not simply a draft riot. It is worth noting that this view is emphatically shared by the Kyrgyz scholar and diplomat Kuban Mambetaliev, who has recently published an important collection of papers on the Uprising drawn from archives within Kyrgyzstan.[2]

2. Ibid., p. 6.

The 1916 Uprising was region-wide in scope, but it assumed a different character in every part of Central Asia. Among the settled peoples of the Ferghana Valley of Uzbekistan, Tajikistan, and Kyrgyzstan (to whom Sokol refers with the old term "Sarts") and on the Merv oasis in Turkmenistan, the focus was on the usurpation of cotton land by Russian settlers and the government's demand that local farmers turn over part of their crop to the state, in addition to paying taxes. They rightly understood that this form of corvée labor was similar to serfdom that had been abolished in Russia. In mountain areas in Kyrgyzstan and East Kazakhstan the Turkic peoples objected to being forced to raise poppies to produce opium needed to treat wounded soldiers on the European front. Religious and national concerns also played a part, although Sokol cautions against overemphasizing these factors.

The common element among all these contributing factors was the relentless usurpation of native lands by Russian settlers and the Russian state and the deep corruption that accompanied it. This process had been going on since the Russians' first appearance in Central Asia. It took the proposed draft and the requisition of ever more meat and cotton from Central Asia to drive the Turkic and Persianate populations into outright rebellion. Or did it? Sokol cites an extensive study by one G. I. Broido, who was a firsthand observer of the Uprising and who reported in detail on what he had seen. Written in September 1916, while the last phase of the Uprising was still under way, Broido acknowledged all the various background factors but then offered a stunning hypothesis, namely, that the tsar's colonial bureaucrats and military leaders *deliberately* fomented the Uprising to justify the seizure of more land from the Kyrgyz, Kazakhs, Uzbeks, Turkmens, and Tajiks. It is worth noting that Broido was a member of the Bolshevik Party that would seize power in Petrograd a year later.

Broido's thesis has recently garnered support from Kuban Mambetaliev, editor of the newly published collection of documents cited above, who republished extracts from it.[3] However, for now this re-

3. Ibid., pp. 257 ff.

mains a hypothesis that must be carefully tested in each of the many regions in which the Uprising welled up. This will require detailed studies of the Uprising of 1916 in each of the countries of the region. Even though Russian officials have closed the main Moscow archives to scholars, there are relevant materials from the tsarist era in the archives in each of the countries of Central Asia, and especially those in Tashkent, Uzbekistan, and Almaty (formerly Vernyi), Kazakhstan. A careful examination of these sources will go far towards establishing whether Russian colonial administrators deliberately fomented the Uprising of 1916 in order to provide a pretext for seizing native lands.

In 2015, President Almazbek Atambayev of the Kyrgyz Republic signed a decree, "On the Centennial of the Tragic Events of 1916." In it he noted that over a long period of time a strict policy of silence had smothered study of the Uprising and suppressed public knowledge of them. The year 2016, he concluded, was the right time to bury the dead, whose bones are still to be found in the bleak mountain passes, and to honor them by reconstructing the history of their lives and the story of their grievous deaths. The decision of Johns Hopkins University Press, together with the Central Asia–Caucasus Institute at Johns Hopkins's Nitze School of Advanced International Studies, to republish Edward Dennis Sokol's valuable monograph is an important step in this direction.

S. Frederick Starr
Chairman
Central Asia–Caucasus Institute
Nitze School of Advanced International Studies
Johns Hopkins University

Preface

The purpose of this study is to serve as an introduction to a period of history which has long suffered from neglect. This must be regarded as something in the nature of a pioneering work rather than a definitive study inasmuch as some of the Russian sources pertinent to the Revolt of 1916 were inaccessible to me despite great efforts to secure them. I am only too well aware that additional light should be shed on many aspects of the revolt in order to obtain a clearer picture.

All dates in this study are in the Old Style of the Russian calendar.

I wish to express my gratitude for the assistance given me by my professors and many colleagues at the Johns Hopkins University, without whose help and cooperation this study would not have been possible.

To Miss Lilly Lavarello goes my great appreciation for doing an excellent job in typing the manuscript in spite of the inherent difficulties of the subject matter. The staff of the History department library at the Johns Hopkins University must be mentioned for the many courtesies and assistance rendered as must the New York Public Library for their dispatch and efficiency in providing photostats of some of the material.

E.D.S.
April 1954

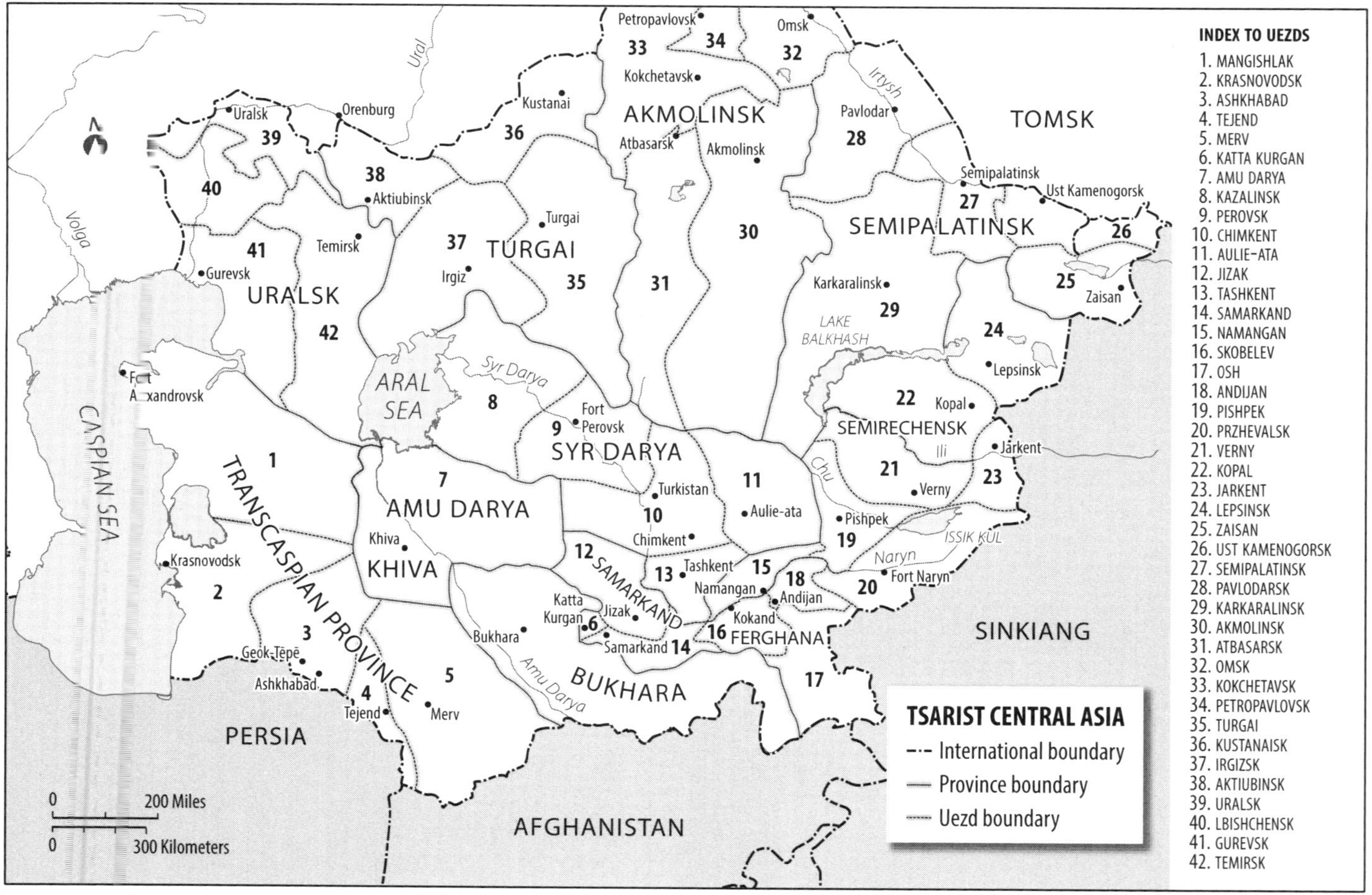
TSARIST CENTRAL ASIA
International boundary
Province boundary
Uezd boundary
INDEX TO UEZDS
1. MANGISHLAK
2. KRASNOVODSK
3. ASHKHABAD
4. TEJEND
5. MERV
6. KATTA KURGAN
7. AMU DARYA
8. KAZALINSK
9. PEROVSK
10. CHIMKENT
11. AULIE-ATA
12. JIZAK
13. TASHKENT
14. SAMARKAND
15. NAMANGAN
16. SKOBELEV
17. OSH
18. ANDIJAN
19. PISHPEK
20. PRZHEVALSK
21. VERNY
22. KOPAL
23. JARKENT
24. LEPSINSK
25. ZAISAN
26. UST KAMENOGORSK
27. SEMIPALATINSK
28. PAVLODARSK
29. KARKARALINSK
30. AKMOLINSK
31. ATBASARSK
32. OMSK
33. KOKCHETAVSK
34. PETROPAVLOVSK
35. TURGAI
36. KUSTANAISK
37. IRGIZSK
38. AKTIUBINSK
39. URALSK
40. LBISHCHENSK
41. GUREVSK
42. TEMIRSK
TOMSK
AKMOLINSK
SEMIPALATINSK
TURGAI
URALSK
SEMIRECHENSK
SYR DARYA
AMU DARYA
KHIVA
SAMARKAND
FERGHANA
BUKHARA
TRANSCASPIAN PROVINCE
SINKIANG
PERSIA
AFGHANISTAN
CASPIAN SEA
ARAL SEA
LAKE BALKHASH
ISSIK KUL
Volga
Ural
Irtysh
Syr Darya
Amu Darya
Chu
Ili
Naryn
Petropavlovsk
Omsk
Kokchetavsk
Kustanai
Uralsk
Orenburg
Atbasarsk
Akmolinsk
Pavlodar
Semipalatinsk
Ust Kamenogorsk
Aktiubinsk
Turgai
Temirsk
Irgiz
Gurevsk
Karkaralinsk
Zaisan
Lepsinsk
Kopal
Jarkent
Verny
Pishpek
Fort Naryn
Fort Perovsk
Turkistan
Aulie-ata
Chimkent
Tashkent
Namangan
Andijan
Kokand
Katta Kurgan
Jizak
Samarkand
Bukhara
Khiva
Krasnovodsk
Geok-Tēpē
Ashkhabad
Tejend
Merv
0 200 Miles
0 300 Kilometers

The Revolt of 1916 in Russian Central Asia

1

The Revolt of 1916

The Revolt of 1916 in Russian Central Asia is an aspect of the history of the First World War and of the history of Russia which has, unfortunately, been sorely neglected in the English literature on the period. Where dealt with at all it receives but casual mention in a paragraph or two at the most. The great attention has been devoted to the February and October Revolutions and the great events attendant upon these upheavals, so œcumenical in their ramifications and significance. Yet the Revolt of 1916 sounded the first rumble of the oncoming disaster and in it there participated in one form or another the eleven million native peoples of Russian Central Asia. Though brutally suppressed, the discontent did not abate but broke out anew in the summer of 1917; the Revolution of October was anticipated in Turkistan by a local coup in September 1917 of the central executive committee of the Tashkent Soviet which overthrew the authorities of the Provisional Government. The Revolt of 1916 was both the prelude to the Revolution in Russia proper and the catalytic agent which hastened the alignment of forces in Russian Central Asia. The Revolution found the lines more sharply drawn and the people more definitely committed to one camp or another than would have been the case had no revolt occurred.

The Revolt of 1916 had still another significance in that it was the final expression of Tsarist policy towards minorities. The revolt is a mirror which in its facets shows the success of the contact and symbiosis of different cultures and different peoples. It provided the acid test which showed how firm these contacts were.

The revolt deserves study for still another reason. It provides an elementary expression of that revolt of Asia against the rule of the white man which is occupying so much of our attention presently. A close corollary to this is the age-long struggle of Islam against the infidel; this also finds its expression in the Revolt of 1916.

Finally, the revolt embodies in the same framework the response of two very different peoples, the nomads and the settled folk, to the encroachment on their liberty and very existence. Each responded in a way consistent with its background, tradition, and history.

In view of the general lack of knowledge about the region of Russian Central Asia or Russian Turkistan it seems pertinent to make a few general remarks about the peoples, their religion, and the land they occupy, before proceeding to the subject proper. The region is a land of great contrast, physically interspersed by desert and oasis, the aspect of the latter heightened by the gloom and desolation of the former. The traveller, exhausted by traversing the desert wastes of Kara Kum and Kizil Kum looks upon such oases as Samarkand and Bukhara, prodigal in verdure, as indeed something out of the Arabian Nights. Water in this region is synonymous with life itself and it alone makes possible the great contrasts between the desert and the cultivated portions of the area. The region of Tsarist Russian Turkistan may be divided into three natural areas: (1) to the west, the province of Transcaspia, composed principally of deserts, whose rivers reach no lake but disappear into the sands; (2) in the centre, the three provinces of Syr Darya, Samarkand, and Ferghana and the khanates of Khiva and Bukhara, vassal to the Russian Government. These units within the Russian Empire were situated in the hydrographic basin of the Sea of Aral, into which flowed the two principal rivers of the country, the Amu Darya and the Syr Darya (the Oxus and Jaxartes of the ancients); (3) to the east, the province of Semirechie, situated in the hydrographic basin of Lakes Balkhash and Issik Kul[1] and the river Chu.

Another great contrast is provided by the variations in level. The steppes and desert of the west are succeeded by the mountains of the east and southeast. Here is found Mt. Kaufmann (now Mt. Stalin) the highest peak in the Soviet Union (23,000 feet) and to the south of it the Pamirs, the "Roof of the World." A final contrast is provided in the matter of population distribution. Whereas in the great cities the population was as dense as in the cities of Europe, in the desert areas it was very sparse.

The name "Turkistan" signifies in Iranian "land of the Turks" yet the name is inaccurate. Inhabited by an Iranian people since time immemorial this population was subjected to a series of conquests, displacements, and interpenetrations by Persians, Greeks, Arabs, Turks, Chinese, Mongols, and others. Though each of these people left its mark, the basic strain of the population remained as before Iranian. The most serious changes in the country were effected by the Arabs and the Turks, the one imposing Mohammedanism on the country and the other the Turkish language.

Of the peoples occupying the area some are of quite pure Iranian provenience, such as the Tajiks, a sedentary people who are especially adept at agriculture. Others are Turko-Mongols, inhabiting their conical *kibitkas* or felt tents and carrying on a nomadic existence. These include the Kirghiz and Kazakhs. In Tsarist times both were called Kirghiz to distinguish them from the Cossacks, the same word being used in Russian to signify Cossack and Kazakh. Where need arose the Kirghiz and Kazakhs were differentiated between by calling the Kazakhs, Kirghiz-Kazakhs and the Kirghiz, Black or Kara Kirghiz.[2] The Kazakhs

1. Issik Kul, literally in Turkic, warm (*issik*) lake (*kul*). To be referred hence simply as Issik Kul.

2. In 1925 the First All-Kazakh Congress of Soviets adopted at Kzil Orda a motion for the change of the word "Kirghiz" to Kazakh in relation to the people inhabiting present-day Kazakhstan. The modern usage is conformed to in this study.

occupied the area of the Kirghiz steppe (now Kazakhstan). The Kirghiz roamed over the region on the T'ien Shan and Pamirs. Both peoples are related in origin, culture, and economy and both pay a nominal allegiance to the Mohammedan religion.

The Turkomans are also Turko-Mongol in race, inhabiting the southwest of Turkistan. They are a hardy nomad people who put up a magnificent resistance to the Russian conquest. Formerly they were much addicted to plundering and made forays to the south as far as Farah, 150 miles south of Herat, bringing back Persian girls for the slave markets of Khiva and Bukhara. These slave girls were married off to the local population further strengthening the Iranian strain of the population. The Turkomans, together with the other nomads, Kirghiz and Kazakhs, made up 30% of the total population of Tsarist Russian Central Asia.

In addition to the pure Iranian strain the sedentary population includes mixtures of the Turko-Mongol and the Iranian. These people inhabit the oases of the east. They include the Sarts[3] and the Uzbeks; the latter are thought to be related to the Seljuk Turks[4] though now containing a heavy admixture of Iranian blood. Both the Sarts and the Uzbeks are industrious and active people.

3. Up to the Revolution, the Russians used the word "Sart" as a general term for urban and settled agricultural inhabitants of Central Asia. The term was usually applied to people who spoke one or another of the Turkish languages or dialects, but also to Iranian-speaking Tajiks. It was not, however, applied to the Chinese-speaking Dungans. Use of the term was discontinued after the Revolution because it was considered derogatory and partly because it prevented use of the true names of nationalities, such as Uzbek. It has been necessary here to retain the term "Sart," however, because it has usually been impossible to determine with precision exactly what people was meant where the term "Sart" is used in the documents on which this study is based.

The most recent authoritative discussion of the term is in Paul Pelliot, *Notes sur l'histoire de la Horde d'Or* (Paris, 1949), p. 34: "Sartaq a abouti à la désignation actuelle des Sart (nos 'Sartes') du Turkestan russe; en réalité, Sartaq est une forme turque, parvenue par l'iranien, qui remonte au skr. sārtha, 'marchand'; le -*q* final peut être dû soit à un dérivé skr. *Sarthaka*, soit à un suffixe iranien."

The term has had a long history and wide travels in Inner Asia; it still survives among the Mongols as a tribal and clan name, in the form Sartagol.

4. Georges Jorré, *The Soviet Union: The Land and Its People* (London and New York, 1950), p. 91.

Mention should also be made of the 228,000 native Jews. Though oppressed by the native governments they prospered much, especially in the cotton trade. They were located notably in Samarkand and Bukhara. With the conquest of Central Asia by the Russians there began an influx of Russian Jews into the country. Other alien elements to come included the Persians, who came as traders, artisans, and workers in great numbers (Ashkhabad was a Persian city), Armenians, and others from the Caucasus who introduced a strong trading element. The problems created by the influx of Russian colonists into the country will be dealt with in a later chapter.

Russian Turkistan does not present a formidable problem in the matter of language, being unlike the Babel of the Caucasus. With the exception of the district of Samarkand and the mountainous parts of the former khanate of Bukhara (present-day Tajikistan) all speak one of several mutually intelligible dialects of the Turkic language. It is in the matter of religion that the differences are most significant. Though the country was predominantly Moslem in faith, the degree of religious fervor varied considerably among the different peoples. Among the sedentary peoples there was no place in the Mohammedan world which was more known for its rigid acceptance of the Koran and of the Sunna dogma, for its many saints and religious orders. Bukhara was regarded by many of the faithful as second only to Mecca in sanctity while its many *medressehs* or religious colleges graduated large numbers of students each year[5] and sent them over Central Asia to carry on the Moslem faith. First introduced in the 10th and 11th centuries to compete with Buddhism, Nestorian Christianity, and animism already long established there, Mohammedanism was closely identified with Iranian culture; Mohammedanism meant the progress of the arts, sciences, literature, and agriculture. This favorable situation changed with the political and economic decline of Turkistan; the country declined considerably after the passing of the Timurides. Wars between

5. As many as 16,000 mullahs were turned out annually. Corliss Lamont, *The Peoples of the Soviet Union* (New York, 1946), p. 107.

the different parts of the region were endemic while the discovery of the Cape of Good Hope route by the Portuguese caused a diversion of the trade routes which affected Turkistan especially. The Russian conquest found a situation that little favored the advancement of civilization and culture. Moslem theologians waged a furious and successful battle against any innovation or alteration in the *status quo*, against anything at variance with the strict tenets of the Koran and the Shariat, the Moslem written law. All instruction was in the hands of the clergy and its jejune and impractical content was directed at the training of clerics true to the most conservative traditions. Law, theology, and a smattering of general knowledge based on traditional lore were the main subjects taught. The world was considered flat, surrounded on all sides by mountains. The pupils repeated in parrot fashion texts from the Arab and Persian classics without ever really learning these languages.[6]

Among the nomads Mohammedanism had but a slight hold on the people in the matter of belief and observance, though the nomad would have resented the imputation that he was not a good Moslem. In the north (Semirechie, Semipalatinsk, Akmolinsk and Uralsk provinces) the acceptance was especially casual, while the Kirghiz and Kazakhs were converted only after the Russian conquest in the 18th and 19th centuries. Oddly enough, the conversion of the Kazakhs from Shamanism to Islam was effected by the Russians themselves. "At first but a few of their sultans and chiefs had any idea of the doctrines of Islam, and there was not a mosque or mullah in the Steppe, but the Russians . . . insisted on treating them as though they were Mohammedans, built mosques and sent mullahs, until the whole people became outwardly Mussulman, although the farther from the Russian lines, and the nearer to the settled population of Central Asia the weaker was the faith."[7] Both among the Kirghiz and Kazakhs and among the Turkomans, the mullahs were given less respect than any-

6. M. A. Czaplicka, *The Turks in History and at the Present Day* (Oxford, 1918), pp 36–37.

7. Eugene Schuyler, *Turkistan* (New York, 1877), vol. I, p. 38.

where else in Mohammedan territory. They rarely prayed and mixed their faith with pagan superstition. The nomad women went about unveiled, unlike the Sart women.

Of all the peoples of Central Asia the Turkomans were the most warlike. They were the last to be conquered and laid down their arms only after the great siege of Geok Tēpē, a huge clay mound built by the Turkomans as their point of final resistance. After breaching the walls by the explosion of land mines the Russians stormed the stronghold. A general massacre took place in which 20,000 men, women, and children are said to have perished.[8]

The resistance put up by the rest of the inhabitants was much less formidable. The Russians, by virtue of their superior armament and discipline, and by profiting by the inveterate hostility among the khanates of Kokand, Khiva, and Bukhara, were able to effect the conquest with small bodies of troops even when faced by armies of great number. The Sarts did not distinguish themselves by the qualities of bravery and valour and were routed by any display of determination by the Russians.

Approached in its international setting the Russian conquest of Central Asia was but part and parcel of the great expansion of the West at the expense of Islam at this time. Everywhere Moslem states were under attack, and by the beginning of Abdul Hamid's reign (1878) only Turkey remained independent although even here the Western Powers were making serious inroads. The Moghul Empire of India, in the sixteenth and seventeenth centuries the equal of the Ottoman Empire, found its quietus in the Indian Mutiny after a dishonorable period of subjection to the East India Company; the British Queen had but recently assumed the title of Empress of India; the Manchu Government

8. Gen. Kuropatkin, who took part in this campaign, asserts that noncombatants were not intentionally harmed and the casualties for the Turkomans were 9,000 out of a total of 30,000. Doubtless many women and children were killed by the rain of petroleum shells on the enclosure before the final assault. F. Skrine and D. Ross, *Heart of Asia: A History of Russian Turkestan and the Central Asian Khanates from the Earliest Times* (London, 1899), pp. 296–297.

had recently crushed the Moslems of Yunnan, Kansu, and the Tarim Basin. Everywhere Islam was on the defensive, politically, psychologically, and culturally.

The reaction of the Western World to the Russian conquest was uniformly favorable—"undoubtedly a piece of constructive action."[9] The suppression of slavery, incessant wars, and anarchy was regarded as a positive achievement of Western civilization as carried forward by Russia. In 1891 the International Geographic Conference lauded "the Rusian people who set up order in Central Asia, who knew how to civilize it, and who developed it."[10] A long series of travellers in the period from the conquest to the First World War penned similar sentiments concerning Russian rule in Central Asia. Even the Russophobe Sir Henry Rawlinson spoke the following words at a meeting of the Royal Geographical Society in 1882:

> No one will question but that the extension of Russian arms to the east of the Caspian has been of immense benefit to the country. The substitution, indeed, of Russian rule for that of the Kirghiz, Uzbegs and Turkomans throughout a large portion of Central Asia has been an unmixed blessing to humanity. The execrable slave trade, with its concomitant horrors, has been abolished, brigandage been suppressed, and Mohametan fanaticism and cruelty have been generally mitigated and controlled. Commerce at the same time has been rendered more secure, local arts and manufactures have been encouraged, and the wants of the inhabitants have been everywhere more seriously regarded than is usual under Asiatic rulers.[11]

Lord George Curzon expressed similar sentiments about the "White Man's Burden" of Russia in Central Asia. What alarmed people like Rawlinson and Curzon was not the Russian conquest of the khanates *per se*—which was all to the good—but the fear that Russia would use

9. See Zeki Velidi Togan, *The Turkistan of Today and Its Recent History* (Istanbul, 1940, and Cairo, 1947) (Turkish and Egyptian editions). Unfortunately, I have not been able to consult this important book but have had access to an abstract in English.

10. Ibid.

11. Quoted by George Curzon, *Russia in Central Asia in 1899 and the Anglo-Russian Question* (London, 1899), p. 384.

her new Asian possessions as a spring-board for further adventures in Afghanistan and India.

Other writers conjured up absurd pictures of future Genghis Khans and Tamerlanes issuing forth with their hordes from Central Asia to engulf Europe in a bath of blood. The German ethnographer, F. Ratzel, stated that "if Nomadism constituted a political danger to Europe the sacred task of keeping it in restraint devolved upon China and Russia." The development of any national feeling or revival among the Moslem peoples was highly suspect and was branded as Pan-Turanianism, Pan-Turkism, or Pan-Islamism to be regarded as more dangerous than any other national movement. Zealots who fought for their religion in Christian countries were termed heroes and saints while such Moslems were labelled fanatics.

Thus it may be seen that Russia found moral support for its rule over the natives of Russian Central Asia from the rest of the Western World. The Moslems of Central Asia could expect little in the way of encouragement, stimulus, and aid from their co-religionists in Africa and the rest of Asia, themselves fighting a losing battle with Western imperialism. The day had not yet come for the emergence of Moslem nationalism or of the modern Pan-Islamic idea. The medieval dirt and picturesqueness remained along with the feckless acceptance of his lot by the native.

2

The Economic Background to the Revolt of 1916

It is generally true that economic causes figure heavily in the explanation of almost all revolts. In few revolts, however, does the economic factor play so conspicuous a role as in the Revolt of 1916. Only a consideration of the many and profound economic changes effected by the coming of the Russians enables one to understand the form of the uprising and the actions of the insurgents.

A. Russian Economic Interests in Central Asia before the Conquest

The first active Russian economic interest in Central Asia may be dated to Peter the Great's reign. Though traditionally pictured as the monarch who oriented Russia to the West, Peter, nevertheless, was greatly interested in the economic potentialities of Asia. Missions were dispatched to China which eventuated in the signing of the Treaty of Kiakhta with China in 1727 just after Peter's death. This treaty gave great advantages to Russia over the other Western powers, establishing permanent commercial relations and a regular diplomatic representation at Peking.[1] The Russian religious mission in Peking pre-

1. V. V. Barthold, *La découverte de l'Asie; Histoire de l'Orientalisme en Europe et en Russie* (Paris, 1947), p. 228. It should be said, however, that the advantages looked better on paper in tonnage of cargo. In spite of all political difficulties one small sailing ship could load more at Canton than several great caravans.

sented a very favorable opportunity for scientific study of China in view of recent edicts against the Jesuits.

Peter's interest in Central Asia was equally great. Here his appetite was aroused by exaggerated visions of gold to be found here and of the supposed practicability of using the Amu Darya as a water route to India by turning the Amu Darya from the Sea of Aral to its old outlet to the Caspian Sea.[2] Expeditions were dispatched but they proved abortive; the mission under Prince Bekovich-Cherkassky was in fact annihilated through the treachery of the Khan of Khiva (1717). Peter's war with Persia gained him, under the treaty of St. Petersburg, 1723, Persia's Caspian provinces, but these were recovered by Persia in a few years. Thus Peter's efforts in Central Asia brought no permanent gain. If more was not accomplished it was not through lack of interest on his part but rather because of his great preoccupation with affairs in the West.

Though preoccupation with Western questions took most of the attention of succeeding Tsarist governments in foreign affairs there was nevertheless a continued interest in Central Asia. With the failure of military expeditions the government adopted other tactics. There began the gradual subjugation of the steppe nomads lying between the Central Asian khanates and Russia proper. The Kazakhs during the first quarter of the eighteenth century had been pressed to the West by the attacks of the Kalmyks or Western Mongols so that they impinged on Russian territory. The Kazakhs were divided at the time into three hordes, the Great, Middle, and Little. Utilizing the quarrels among them the Russian government succeeded in 1732 by gifts and bribery during the reign of the Empress Anne in persuading the Khan of the Little Horde to accept Russian suzerainty. Similar policies towards the Middle and Great Hordes resulted by the end of the 1740s in the annexation of the territories of Turgai, Uralsk, and part of Semipalatinsk and Akmolinsk. These territories provided a base for further penetration into Central Asia.

2. Op. cit., p. 235.

The first half of the nineteenth century saw the Russians strengthening their influence over the western part of the steppe. In 1822 new laws were enacted for the administration of the Kazakhs. The privileges of the Sultans or chieftains were circumscribed while a certain degree of autonomy was granted to the Kazakhs. In the view of the Russians peace in the steppe could only be secured by the breaking of the power of the leader over the clan, the traditional organization of the Kazakhs. This was effected by the creation of administrative units which did not correspond with clan divisions but cut across these lines.[3]

Though the Kazakhs were now Russian subjects, conditions in the steppe were, if anything, more turbulent than before. The common people (black bones) still had great respect for their aristocracy (white bone—the expression equivalent to "blue blood" in a number of Inner Asian societies). The marauding proclivities of the Kazakhs were still strong and any "*batyr*" or hero was certain to find a following.[4] The Sultans recognized by the Russians could not keep order or did not want to while the annual military expeditions from Orenburg (now Chkalov) proved equally ineffectual. Only with the establishment of strongholds in strategic positions in the steppes by Governor-General Obruchev (1845), advances on the Syr Darya, the overthrow of the brigand Isetz Kutebarof, and the demise of the batyr, Jan Hodja, brought peace to the steppe,[5] and facilitated the dispatch into the steppes of Russian caravans. The occupation of Aralskoe in 1847 on the lower Syr Darya marked the beginning of a new period—the Russian encroachment on the Central Asian khanates and their conquest.

3. Barthold, op. cit., p. 274. Cf. Manchu empire's policy towards Mongols. See O. Lattimore, "Mongolia," *China Year Book*, 1933, p. 193.

4. When the pastoral economy is dislocated by new forms of administrative control, trade, and—especially—colonization, the bolder spirits among the tribesmen are apt to strike back by "going on the war-path." Hence they are described as "marauders" by their civilized conquerors, who eventually write the history of what happened. Cf. the American folk-historical picture of the Indians as "people who tried to drive out the white man."

5. Schuyler, op. cit., vol. I, p. 32.

Russia's trade with Asia did not attain great proportions during the first half of the nineteenth century; in general only 6–7% and not over 10% of all her exports passed over her Asiatic borders. This fact, however, obscures the real significance of her trade. While Russia's exports to Europe were predominantly raw materials and half manufactured goods her Asiatic exports included a significant proportion of manufactured goods.[6]

While the Persian and Transcaspian trade grew more rapidly than the trade with the Central Asian khanates in the first quarter of the century, by the middle of the 1830s the situation had changed. There was a significant drop in Russia's Iranian trade as a result of the development of a new trade route to Iran via Turkey and the introduction there of English textiles. It is in this setting that the Central Asian market assumes great importance.

The articles imported were for the most part raw cotton, cotton yarn, and fabrics. The unfavorable trade balance for Russia was settled by gold while fabrics, sugar, tableware, and other goods were exported to Central Asia.[7] Russian cotton textile manufacture benefited especially by this trade. In 1840, 73% of all cotton stuffs sent to Asia were taken by the Central Asian market.[8] In this trade, which had been carried on through the intermediary of Khivan and Bukharan merchants, direct trade relations were entered into in 1840. The Russian manufacturers showed a great knack, starting about 1828 and 1829, in manufacturing articles that would suit the taste of the Asian market. In the matter of clothing, travellers were to have a difficult time in distinguishing between native productions and Russian imitations. As in India, the influx of cheap foreign cotton stuff was to doom native production to extinction.

According to the figures of one authority Russian trade with Central Asia was evaluated at 10.53 million roubles for the decade 1827–

6. M. K. Rozhkova, "Russkie fabrikanty i rynki srednego vostoka vo vtoroi chetverti XIX veka," *Istoricheskie zapiski*, no. 27 (1948), p. 144.

7. P. Lyashchenko, *History of the National Economy of Russia to the 1917 Revolution* (New York, 1949), p. 354.

8. Rozhkova, op. cit., p. 155.

1837 and 15.73 million roubles for 1840–1850.[9] While the export of cloth and other goods to Central Asia continued to grow increasingly, the import of cotton increased even more in volume. Thus in the decade 1857–1867 imports to Russia rose almost 4.4 times while exports from Russia rose 2.14 times.[10] The decade 1857–1867 shows a colossal increase in trade; the turnover in this period was 946% greater than in the decade 1840–1850.

Thus as an economic background for the conquest of Central Asia we see the very rapid development of trade with Central Asia. The mills of Moscow and Lodz were relying increasingly on the coarse, short-staple cotton of Turkistan while they saw in Central Asia a preserve for the sale of their cotton stuffs.

The period of the conquest (the 1860s) saw a wild bacchanalia of speculation, coal and oil scandals in which even the military were involved. The potentialities and richness of the country were much exaggerated and most of the Russian ventures that were started in these years failed in the early '70s. Though of importance to the Russian manufacturers the local cotton was wretched in quality and the great demand was not to come until the early 1880s when American Upland cotton was introduced.

B. Russian Economic Policy towards the Sarts

1. Land Policy

When the Russians came to Central Asia, landholding was nominally regulated according to the Shariat or Moslem religious law. Nominally all land was the sole possession of the State. In actuality this principle was modified through custom (*adat*) and local conditions, and a confused situation existed. Land was classified in three major categories: (1) *amlyak*—land belonging to the state. This included most of the uncultivated land, the land used by the nomads, and such land as was cultivated by private persons paying certain fees. In practice these

9. P. G. Galuzo, *Turkestan—Koloniya (Ocherk istorii Turkestana ot zavoe-vaniya russkimi do revolyutsii 1917 goda)* (Moscow, 1929), p. 8.

10. Ibid., p. 8.

lands might be classed as private property inasmuch as the occupier could dispose of it; (2) *mulk*—land in private ownership given by the state in return for service; (3) *vakuf*—land given to some mosque or religious school either by the State or by some private individual.[11]

The Russian government revived the concept of the Shariat that all land belonged to the state. Though it left the Sarts in possession of the land they already occupied, all uncultivated land was listed as belonging to the government. At the time of the coming of the Russians the system of landholding was terribly confused thanks to the venality of the officials, local custom, and lack of documents. The Russian government cut this Gordian knot by subjecting all land to the same tax (except the vakuf lands) thus removing many inequalities.

In the extremely vital matter of irrigation the Russian government left the system in the hands of the natives though reserving the right of general supervision and to make all future extensions in the irrigation systems. According to customary law (adat) there was no private property in water; an equal distribution was to be made among all the lands. In practice many abuses and inequalities resulted. To assure equal distribution all land had to be absolutely level, a matter which required a tremendous amount of labor. Often the control of the water was monopolized by some powerful personage who favored the rich and collected bribes from the agriculturists. Regions downstream were often left short of water; thus Bukhara, downstream on the Zarafshan river, often received less water than the Samarkand region; the canals and installations were makeshift affairs and the water often broke through the banks of the canal. By the end of the Tsarist era new installations were extremely modest in extent though Tsarist engineers had great plans for the future.

2 The Introduction of American Cotton

The growing of cotton in Turkistan goes back to antiquity having been introduced from India via Afghanistan and Persia. It was the

11. Lyashchenko, op. cit., p. 606; Schuyler, op. cit., vol. I, pp. 298–299.

short-staple variety, coarse, and requiring double labor inasmuch as the pods did not open as widely as the American variety and hence had to be picked from the shrub before the cotton could be taken out.[12] Russian manufactures took more and more of the native cotton though they preferred to import American cotton. Caravans of cotton went to Russia generally by the Orenburg route. A great impetus was given to this importation by the great rise in cotton prices during the American Civil War, reaching fabulous proportions in 1863. Thus if we take cotton prices in the United States in 1900 at 100 we get the following table for the years 1859–1865.

1859	118	1862	723
1860	139	1863	1091
1861	336	1864	972
		1865	462[13]

This record price period is followed by one of an almost uninterrupted lowering of prices until 1885. The introduction of American cotton seed into Turkistan in the early 1880s by Governor-General Kaufman was a moment of tremendous significance for the future of the country. This introduction coincided with a renewed climbing of cotton prices after 1885.[14]

1885	101	1888	115
1886	110	1889	124
1887	110		

At the same time the building of the Transcaspian railway was being pushed forward, which was to connect all the important cities of Russian Central Asia. In 1884, it was brought to Merv, in 1886 to

12. A. Meakin, *In Russian Turkestan: A Garden of Asia and Its People* (London, 1915), p. 31.

13. Galuzo, op. cit., p. 17.

14. Ibid., p. 18.

the Amu Darya and in 1888 to Samarkand (later to Tashkent and from there to Orenburg). Though conceived of as a strictly military measure by military men, its character soon changed and it became a going commercial undertaking. The railway brought a lowering of cotton transportation costs, a tying of the economy to the fluctuations of the world market and the conversion of Turkistan into a cotton colony of the Tsarist Empire. A few statistics will illustrate the great growth of cotton of the American variety.[15]

Turkistan Cotton Exports to Russia

1888	873,000 puds[16]
1889	1,470,000 "
1890	2,673,000 "
1890–96	4,300,000–4,900,000 puds
1907	10,700,000 puds

Tashkent was the northern limit and Andijan the eastern of the growth of this crop. The "cotton fever" especially gripped the Ferghana province comprising about two-thirds of the total cotton acreage. The working up of various cotton products took 60% of all labor in Ferghana, 80% of all mechanical power, 80% of all fuel, and 92% of the total figure of the production of the *oblast*.[17] The other basic oblasts registered the following increase in the cotton harvest for the years 1908 to 1913:[18]

Syr Darya	210.8%
Samarkand	46.5%

15. Lyashchenko, op. cit., p. 610–611. It is significant to note that while cotton production rose to 14 million puds by the eve of World War I the importation of foreign cotton (chiefly Amercian) remained at 10 million puds, showing no decrease. See Boris L. T. Roustam-Bek, "First Mohammedan Republic," *Asia*, May 1920, p. 391.

16. A pud = 36.11 lbs.

17. Georgii Safarov, *Kolonialnaya revolyutsia (opyt turkestana)* (Moscow, 1921), p. 39.

18. Ibid., p. 38.

Cotton was also grown in the Transcaspian region around Merv, but not in Semirechie.

Great as was the obsession with cotton in these years it was dwarfed by the grandiose plans put forward in the last years of Tsarism. Senator Count Palen in the year 1906 made an intensive official examination of the state of the country and reported that the natural boundary for the extension of cotton growing (325,000 dessiatines) had already been reached. On the other hand, Krivoshein, Minister of Agriculture and Stolypin's *alter ego* in his land policies, thought this was but a third of the area that should be irrigated and put to cotton growing. The water system of the Amu Darya alone was declared to be almost comparable to the Nile, while "Each extra pud of Turkistan wheat is competition for Russian and Siberian wheat; every extra pud of Turkistan cotton is competition for American cotton"—so Krivoshein states in a memorial. Taking a leaf from the history of Egypt—the first big example of a monoculture satisfying its food requirements from the outside—Krivoshein seized upon this concentration as a desideratum for Turkistan. The region was to abandon its grain and rice culture altogether for a single devotion to the growing of cotton. It was in this connection that he conceived the idea of the Turkistan-Siberian (Turk-Sib) railway—usually thought of as a Soviet conception—as facilitating the export of Siberian grain into the region. The years of 1911–1913 saw construction started from both ends. The work was hampered by lack of capital and the increased attention given to the menacing situation in the West. Though the war brought an end to this construction, 1915 saw the completion of the stretch from Novosibirsk to Semipalatinsk.[19] All the technical problems had been worked out. Only some bridges remained to be put up.[20]

And what of the *dekhan*—the native peasant—in the feverish race to make cotton King? What was his share in the immense wealth which was being paid out for cotton, and was his life richer or poorer thereby?

19. See Karl Stählin, *Russisch-Turkestan, Gestern und Heute* (Berlin, 1935), pp. 15–16.
20. Lt. Col. F. M. Bailey, *Mission to Tashkent* (London, 1946), p. 45.

On the surface it would appear that the peasant must surely gain in this cotton boom. The secured sale of cotton, duties on American cotton, tax privileges for cotton lands, the predominance of cotton-growing on small native farms rather than on Russian-owned plantations, thus leaving the proceeds of the harvest in the country—all this seemed to point to a better life for all the classes of the population. In actuality the situation of the dekhan became, if anything, much worse.

Though cotton growing was very remunerative it was also subject to great fluctuation not only as to harvest but as to price. Since the United States was by far the major producer of this commodity it virtually set the price by its crop. A bad harvest in Turkistan which coincided with a good one in the United States (with the lowering of the price of cotton) meant a catastrophe for the grower in Turkistan.[21] But the grower could not always turn to the raising of food crops inasmuch as the building of the Transcaspian railways brought in the foodstuffs at prices often below the cost of production in Turkistan. In reality the peasant had no choice in the matter as he was given grain only in proportion to the quantity of cotton he produced.[22]

The small cotton grower was placed in a position of dependence upon the metropolitan market for the sale of his crops. Agents of the cotton textile mills and the cotton ginners advanced him a small deposit towards his future crop and from then on his dependence was assured and he sank more and more into debt. Until the beginning of the World War the difference between fall and spring prices for grain and other agricultural commodities reached 50%.[23] The peasant was forced to sell his harvest when prices were low and to buy grain and seeds for sowing in the spring when prices had greatly advanced.[24] To

21. A. Woeikof, *Le Turkestan Russe* (Paris, 1914), p. 258.

22. Bailey, op. cit., p. 45.

23. Safarov, op. cit., p. 34.

24. This was by no means confined to Russian Turkistan. For Russia proper see M. Dobb, *Soviet Economic Development since 1917* (New York, 1948), p. 44. It is also true of China and, in general, countries where the farmer has little working capital, and where tenantry is largely on a share-cropping, rather than a monetary basis.

obtain money for the latter he had to sell even his draught animals and household utensils as well as to have recourse to the usurer.

The Russian investigator, N. Koryton, described the activities of the usurer, in 1904, in the following manner.

> These "benefactors" help the native peasant in the moment of his greatest need by lending him a small sum at an enormous interest, not less than four per cent per month. The transaction takes place before a common judge, and in the debtor's note the interest is always added to the sum borrowed. That is, if the sum of a hundred roubles is borrowed for one year, the note is made out for 148 roubles. Furthermore, if the usurer doubts the debtor's paying capacity, he takes as security a mortgage on the debtor's real property, at the same rate of interest as above and at a valuation of half the property's actual worth. Foreclosures of such mortgages are the usual thing here. Russian usurers have acquired vast tracts of land at the expense of the ruined native peasants.[25]

Taxes were yet another factor that forced the peasant into desperate economic straits. The budget of Turkistan showed a deficit for every year of the prewar era but this only led the government to raise taxes more and more. Inasmuch as the taxes levied did not raise the productive power of the peasantry the result could only be prejudicial to the interests of the latter. Much land was forfeited due to the inability of the peasant to pay the taxes.[26]

Thus via loans from cotton agents, usurers, the increased population pressure on the land, the enhanced price of land due to cotton bringing speculation, increased taxes, the destruction of the self-sufficient village economy through the flood of cheap Russian goods, the peasant sank more and more into indebtedness and lost his land.

Despite the increasing concentration of land in the hands of the rich the peasant usually remained on the plot of land he had lost, farming it on a sharecrop basis. The owner provided the seeds, implements, and the land while the tenant did all the work. The crop was divided between the two, the owner getting the lion's share. Though

25. Quoted in Joshua Kunitz, *Dawn over Samarkand* (New York, 1935), p. 34.
26. Galuzo, op. cit., p. 37.

the plantation system was introduced it did not prove very successful. Turkistan was for the most part a land of small-scale agriculture, the average independent cotton grower having but from 2 to 4 dessiatines which he cultivated intensively with his crude implements, the *ketman* (hoe) and the *omach* (native plow). One authority explains the failure of the plantation system in terms of the psychological reaction of the peasant; when working for his family at home he was most industrious but when working for someone else he was disposed to see no sin in loafing or pretending to work.[27]

The expropriation of the peasant's land did not lead to his employment in industry as in Europe and Japan. Russia looked upon this region as a colonial area to serve as a source of raw materials and an outlet for her manufactures. Naturally she could not look with favor upon any great development of industry there.[28]

The situation among the *bais* or rich natives was quite different. Not being dependent upon loans they could prosper at cotton growing. They were enlisted as agents of the cotton firms and ginners while to this they added the function of usurer. The increasing closeness of the alliance between the native merchant and the Russians was especially remarked in Tashkent and Samarkand and in the cities of Ferghana. The establishment of the Cotton Exchange at Kokand also contributed to this. Native merchants visited with ever increasing frequency the fair at Nizhni Novgorod and especially Moscow where they founded important native trading companies.[29] Thus by the beginning of the World War rich natives and Russians found much in common, though social intercourse stopped at the native threshold.

3. The Russians in Turkistan

The coming of the Russians to Turkistan differed significantly from that of the British into India. The British came as governors, administrators, and merchants but did not enter into competition with

27. Ibid., p. 20.
28. Kunitz, op. cit., p. 35.
29. Woeikof, op. cit., p. 333.

the natives in other fields. Russians in Turkistan, however, were found in the entire gamut of occupations, from the ruling classes to lavatory cleaners and street sweepers. Thus they entered into competition for jobs with the natives at every level.

Especially galling for the natives was the industrial situation. In the few industries that existed before the war (especially cotton-ginning processing and cottonseed extraction comprising 85% of the industrial production of Turkistan[30]) the Russians monopolized the skilled positions while the natives worked at the rest. But this was not all; the tremendous disparity between the pay and working conditions of the two must also be noted. The natives worked 10 to 12 hours a day and at times 16 hours while their pay averaging 180 roubles a year contrasted very unfavorably with the 288 rouble average for Russia.[31] The outlook for the Russians was quite different. Possessed usually of more mechanical skill than the natives they were a small contingent in Turkistan while further recruitment in Russia proper was beset with many difficulties. In the last years of Tsarism nowhere, perhaps, in the empire were they given such concessions and favorable treatment. The work day was cut to 8 hours in most cases, full rest on holidays, free medical assistance from the employer and pay for interruption in the work without previous notice by the employer.[32] They formed 22.8% of the total industrial labor force while 70–79% were skilled workers.[33]

The railways were the great stronghold of this skilled élite requiring more qualified professional workers than elsewhere. The distribution here was as follows: Russians, 80.7%; Moslems, 14.6%; Poles, 2.6%; Germans, 0.8%; Armenians, 0.7%; Jews, 0.2%.[34]

Russian colonization in the three basic provinces of Turkistan (Syr

30. Ibid., p. 617.

31. Lyashchenko, op. cit., p. 615.

32. Safarov, op. cit., p. 39.

33. Lyashchenko, op. cit., p. 617; A. M. Pankratova and A. L. Sidorov (Editors), *Revolyutsia 1905–1907 godov v natsionalnikh raionakh Rossii. Sbornik statei* (State Printing-house of Political Literature, 1949), p. 520.

34. Safarov, op. cit., p. 41.

Darya, Ferghana, Samarkand) was not great. In 1914 the Russian colonists were distributed thus:[35]

Province	No. of villages	No. of inhabitants
Syr Darya	108	45,000
Samarkand	13	3,500
Ferghana	23	20,000

The Russian peasant cared little for the cultivation of cotton and rice and hence was not much attracted to the region. When there he grew his traditional crops of cereals and fodder. Russians were settled in villages apart from the natives on lands newly opened by irrigation. Their portions were huge by comparison with native standards (often 40–50 dessiatines) but they could not work the land as intensively as the native peasant did with his ketman. Even so the difference between the two was great and the Turkistan Russian peasant prospered while the native worker became further enslaved.

C. Russian Economic Policy towards the Nomads

If the great changes effected by the Russians among the sedentary peoples of Turkistan centred upon the conversion of the country into a cotton province of the Tsarist Empire, among the nomads the story is one of the steady encroachment of the Russian settlers upon the lands of the nomads. The agrarian question then is the touchstone of the relations of the nomads to the Russians.

In the area of present-day Kazakhstan Russians appeared as far back as the sixteenth century. They became much transformed by intermarriage and could be hardly distinguished from the steppe-dweller. The first settlers were soldiers rather than peasants and so the situation was to remain for a long time. They were given great tracts of land and their settlements formed a line of defense against the forays of the wild nomads. There was not yet a single peasant colony in

35. Woeikof, op. cit., p. 305.

1868.[36] The year 1875 marked a change in the settlement of the country after the Governor-General of the Steppes affirmed that the Cossack settlements brought little in the way of civilization to the steppes. It is this year which marks the beginning of peasant colonization of the steppe. In Semirechie, the scene of the most bitter resistance in the Revolt of 1916, the colonization was begun shortly after the conquest of the territory (1867).

In the territories of both the Kazakh and the Kirghiz, colonization at first went ahead leisurely and painlessly for the population. It was not of a mass character and officials like General Kolpakovsky, Governor of Semirechie, approached the question of the seizure of nomad land cautiously. In Semirechie the majority of settlements were formed with the willing consent of the Kirghiz communities.[37]

From the end of the nineteenth century to the beginning of the twentieth century there was a transitional period. Officials like General Kolpakovsky who, though often insufficiently trained, strove to do their best, were now replaced by administrators of lesser moral qualities. Along with this went a stepped-up colonization program and an increasing disregard of the rights of the nomads to land. These tendencies were pushed to their extreme in the period 1905–1916.

In understanding the background for this peasant colonization movement into Russian Central Asia and Siberia a few remarks are pertinent concerning the agrarian situation in Russia. Russian immigration into Asiatic Russia before the Emancipation of the serfs (1861) was necessarily very limited inasmuch as the serfs were bound to the land and were the property of the landholder. The emancipation of the serfs brought an acceleration of the immigration into Asiatic Russia but even here the peasant encountered many obstacles to his free movement. Freed of the control of the lord he was now subjected to the control of the *obshchina* or commune. The collective responsibility of the latter for the payment of taxes, furnishing of recruits for

36. *Handbook of Siberia and Arctic Russia* (Great Britain Admiralty, 1918), vol. I, p. 200.

37. G. I. Broido, "Materialy k istorii vosstaniya kirghiz v 1916 g.," *Novy Vostok*, no. 6 (1924), p. 409.

the army, and payment for the land given them by the Emancipation[38] created an interest in keeping all members of the commune in place so that the obligations on the others would not be increased. The domestic serfs were set free without any land.

The end of the nineteenth century found the Russian government turning its attention more and more to the colonization of Russian Asia by peasant settlers as a means to help solve the critical agrarian problem created since the Emancipation. In the black soil region of Russia the "poverty lots" were imposed upon the peasants by the nobles because of the great value of the land there. A great class of peasantry was created which was forced to hire themselves out as their land was wholly insufficient for providing their needs. While the period registered a movement on the part of the nobles to sell their land to the peasantry this brought little relief inasmuch as the population had grown greatly in the meantime.[39] Between 1860 and 1897 the peasant population of European Russia had grown by more than half. The peasant could only escape redemption payment and communal control by accepting a "poverty lot" of one-fourth of the amount of land he tilled before the Emancipation in which case the peasant had too little land to make a living on. The great peasant disturbances in 1902 followed by the Revolution of 1905 brought great pressure upon the government to seek some sort of solution of the land problem. Asiatic Russia beckoned as a partial answer to this problem. The government was aided in its colonization program by the inauguration of the Transsiberian railway (1891) which played a great part from the very first in bringing the settler to Asiatic Russia. This is the background to the third period of colonization of the Steppe beginning in 1905.

The formation of the Resettlement Administration in 1905 brought in its train not only the rapid colonization of what is now Kazakhstan and Kirghizia but the complete ignoring of the interest of the natives and the ruin of the herding economy.

38. This payment represented not only the price of the land but the redemption of feudal obligations to the lord.

39. Dobb, op. cit., p. 54.

Since the conquest the natives were looked upon as not possessing the land; adopting the rules of the Shariat the government declared all land belonged to it and the nomads were to utilize the land only by the sufferance of the government. It set aside portions for the use of the nomads and declared the rest "surplus," to be taken over by the government as a reserve for future Russian colonization. This was done under the terms of the Steppe *polozhenie* or code, article 120 of which declared that all land which may be termed surplus comes under the jurisdiction of the department of Agriculture. Article 126 stated that the term "surplus lands" meant only those lands which were not necessary to the Kirghiz economy.

The actions of the Resettlement Administration were in violation both of the spirit and the letter of the law. The meaning of the term "surplus land" was given a wider and wider interpretation.[40]

From 1896 to 1902 there was dispatched the first special expedition into the present Kazakhstan area under F. Shcherbin with the goal of finding out the presence and quantity of "surplus lands" and the establishing of "normalized measures" for the partition of land among the local population. The expedition in the years 1896–1902 examined twelve *uezds* (districts) of three oblasts (provinces) of Kazakhstan and found in only eight uezds 22,512,000 dessiatines of "surplus lands."[41]

The Shcherbin expedition was to provide the Resettlement Administration with experience in establishing new norms. The norms established by the Shcherbin expedition were declared too high and new expeditions were dispatched after 1907. The result of all this was an even further lowering of the norm of land declared necessary for the nomads.

In addition the local officials were instructed by St. Petersburg to earmark new lands as "surplus" to be included in the reserve for future colonization. An active competition was begun among the offi-

40. The same held true in the Chinese colonization of Mongol land. See O. Lattimore, *The Mongols of Manchuria* (New York, 1934), p. 107.

41. O. A. Vaganov, "Zemelnaya politika tsarskogo pravitelstva v Kazakhstane," *Istoricheskie zapiski*, no. 31 (1950), p. 71.

cials in this matter while the director of resettlement affairs, Beletsky, instructed them as to the number of dessiatines of surplus land they must register in order to move ahead in the service. One over-zealous official, Mazurenko, went so far as to include a portion of China in the tracts he earmarked for seizure as surplus lands![42] Many higher officials who fulfilled the instructions of St. Petersburg with insufficient vigor were removed. This fate befell Leontev, the vice-governor of the Turgai province in 1906 after he warned the authorities about the danger of creating a mass movement among the Kazakhs and acted against the expropriation of their lands, pointing out that "the police forces do not in any way correspond to the needs and intensity of the same resettlement movement." Later the same fate befell Tomachevsky, the Governor of Turgai province.[43]

Not content with seizing all nomad land outside the established norms the Resettlement Administration in some places sought to place all the best lands in the category of "surplus" while leaving the deserts, hill tops, and scrublands for the nomads. Land was seized even of those Kirghiz and Kazakhs who had adopted a sedentary life and were making a living as agriculturists.[44]

Another dire threat to the nomads was the outright seizure of the water resources by the settlers in a region where water was a matter of life-and-death importance. This was especially pronounced in Semirechie where irrigated agriculture was much developed.

The settlement of the land by the Russians meant not only the taking away of the nomad land but created barriers to the herds of the nomads in their various migrations.

The Resettlement Administration was not the only government agency threatening the nomads. Equally menacing were the activities of the Forest Administration. This agency regarded the forests as the "sole

42. Broido, op. cit., p. 411.

43. Vaganov, op. cit., p. 73.

44. A. V. Shestakov, "Vosstanie v Srednei Azii 1916 g.," *Istorik Marksist*, no. 2 (1926), p. 96. For a comparable situation in regard to the Chinese seizure of Mongol lands, see Lattimore, op. cit., pp. 103–105.

property of the Treasury." What was comprehended by the term "forest" was truly remarkable, often including areas where there was not one tree.

The nomads pressed to the hills by the Resettlement Administration were hounded from there by the Forest Administration. Thus the nomads were caught between two fires.[45]

The nomads were not even afforded protection against squatters. When these people illegally occupied nomad territory their occupation was legalized by the Resettlement Administration despite the complaints of the natives.[46]

The natural increase in population among the Cossack *stanitsas* or villages brought fresh demands for nomad land. A notable example of this is afforded by the case of the Verny Cossack stanitsa in 1915. The normal partition was 30 dessiatines per soul (100–150 dessiatines per family) which was too large for the owner to work. The surplus was rented out to Kirghiz and Kazakhs to work. The increase in population caused the Military Governor of Semirechie, Governor Folbaum, to demand that the adjacent Kirghiz land be added to the partitions even though this meant the ejection of 3,500 Kirghiz families leading a settled agricultural existence there. The final decision was not given in this case but presumably was only interrupted by the outbreak of the Revolution.[47]

The government in its policies was careful to differentiate between the poor and the bais[48] and local native officials, the natural leaders of the people. Bribes and the allotment of large areas of land to the bais and native officials kept the latter on the side of the government. Though the pasture lands formally belonged to the whole community the bais and officials used their wealth and official position to arrogate large tracts to their exclusive control and use.[49]

45. Vaganov, op. cit., p. 75.

46. Broido, op. cit., p. 411.

47. Ibid., p. 412.

48. *Bai*, a Turkish word (properly an adjective) meaning "rich." In Central Asia the word is often added to the name of a prosperous influential person to distinguish him from the mass of people.

49. As with the nomads of Central Asia the Mongols recognized only the ownership of the whole tribe over territory. The renting of Mongol land to Chinese farmers during

The official policy of the government was to foster the transition from a nomad to a sedentary life. To this end they offered a tax exemption for the first five years and half payment of taxes for the succeeding five years to those nomads who would make the transition. The poor nomads were inclined to make the transition as it meant the securing of a portion (even if small) of land free both of Russian and bai, and the adoption of a more progressive form of economy (agriculture). The nomads feared as well that their herding land would be subject to further expropriation. It is significant that the majority of the petitions for transition came from those areas where expropriation was carried through in its most blatant form (Semirechie oblast, the Aktiubinsk and Kustanaisk uezds or districts of the Turgai oblast, the Uralsk and Temirsk uezds of the Uralsk oblast).[50]

The bais, on the other hand, opposed conversion. They owned large herds and feared that conversion might lead to expropriation of their land. In addition they would lose their authority over the people. Thus they used every method of persuasion, including coercion and even murder, to stop these petitions.

The official government position was the following: (1) the nomads, in passing from nomadism to agriculture, will be introduced to a much higher culture; (2) the transition to a sedentary state was advertised as the final agrarian legislation after which all expropriation will come to an end; (3) the government protects the poor against the seizure of land by the bai upper class and assures them of a portion of land in sole and undivided ownership.[51]

In all this we see the characteristic prejudice of agricultural peoples against the nomad and the belief in the superiority of the seden-

---

the Manchu dynasty brought a change. Though the income from land rentals was a tribal fund to be divided among the ruling prince, the officials and the tribe as a whole the privileged class among the Mongols, through their management of funds, profited the most. Tracts of tribal land were recognized by the Chinese authorities as belonging to the Mongol privileged classes in return for the latter's support in expropriating the rest of the tribal territory as "surplus." See Lattimore, op. cit., chapter III.

50. Vaganov, op. cit., p. 78.

51. Ibid., p. 77.

tary life. The same policy was advocated towards the steppe nomad as was carried out against the American Indian; he was to be driven off into the desert and his place taken by "reliable Russian people." The steppe seemed limitless and it was thought the process could be carried on for a long time before the nomads would feel the pinch. What was forgotten was that while summer pastures were plentiful winter pastures were not. The seizure of well-protected and well-watered spots by the Russians doomed the nomads and their flocks to face the full rigours of the steppe winter.[52] The inclusion of hay fields as "forest" by the Forest Administration was equally prejudicial to the nomad's survival while the increasing encroachment of the Russian on the land denied him alternative and supplementary areas in years of drought.[53]

The Russian trader brought vodka, cigarettes, lacquered boots, and other articles of civilization to the nomad breaking down his natural economy and increasing his wants while at the same time the income of the latter was shrinking as his herds decreased in size owing to Russian encroachment on his pasture lands. Semirechie saw the intrusion of the great trading firms of Central Russia with the setting up of trading posts with travelling agents and intermediaries. In 1907 these centres numbered 320. This network penetrated into the most remote *aul* or nomad village of the nomad territory. In addition to the Russians there appeared Uzbek merchants, Tartars, and others. A great business in usury arose alongside this trading as the nomads often had no ready cash. Both operations were carried on by the trader. A glimpse of the way in which these speculators operated is given in the "Agricultural Survey of Semirechie oblast" for the year 1914:

52. The practice of spending winters in the same place appears to be an ancient and general one among Central Asian nomads. Owen Lattimore, *High Tartary* (Boston, 1930), p. 243 ff.; idem. 40, 73 ff.; Alfred E. Hudson, "The Social Structure of the Kazakhs," *Yale University Publications in Anthropology*, no. 20 (New Haven, 1928), p. 30.

53. The nomad does not wander aimlessly but in a well defined circuit. The circuit is usually not great while among the mountain nomads it may be very short. Thus the Kaying Kirghiz of Sinkiang, who are mountain nomads, move a total annual distance of but 10 miles. C. P. Skrine, *Chinese Central Asia* (Boston and New York, 1926), p. 153.

> Such a speculator settled down somewhere in places of the greatest concentration of Kirghiz and handed out goods all winter, for the most part on credit, until the spring; in the spring the debtors were obliged to leave in a determined place for the payment of their debt either live cattle or the products of herding needed by the speculator. In the spring, gathering in such a manner herds of live cattle or transports of pastoral raw materials, the speculators either go to the great fairs farther away to sell these products or send them directly to railway stations for delivery farther on. In the last few years agencies of great Russian firms have appeared in the limits of the oblast for the buying of skins, wool, but these agencies buy only through the speculators, not receiving small parties from the immediate economies.[54]

In such a manner each year at least 14–15% of the livestock of Semirechie left the oblast.

Statistics paint a distressing picture of the circumstances of the nomads in the years just preceding the Revolt. Among the Kirghiz there was created a landless proletariat hiring themselves out for labor; 50% of the Russian settlers in Kirghizia hired *batraks* or native hired hands while the *manaps* or native aristocracy also hired them.[55] By 1913 about 4.5 million hectares of the best agricultural land in Kirghizia had been seized. The driving of the Kirghiz into the deserts and hills brought a drop in the quantity of cattle of 27% in only five years (1902–1907) while the population decreased by 7 to 10% in ten years (1903–1913).[56] The nomad was possessed of land too poor for agriculture and insufficient for herding.[57]

Despite the fact that they were newcomers not enjoying the high protection of the Tsar even the Dungans and Taranchi prospered more

54. Quoted by S. Brainin and S. Shafiro, *Vosstanie kazakhov Semirechya v 1916 godu* (Alma-Ata and Moscow, 1936), p. 5.

55. Introduction: T. R. Ryskulov: *Vosstanie 1916 g.v Kirgizstane: Dokumenty i Materialy sobrannye L. V. Lesnoi. Pod redaktsiei i s predsloviem T. R. Ryskulov* (Moscow, 1937), p. 5 (?).

56. A. Zorin, "Kirgizskaya Sovetskaya Sotsialisticheskaya Respublika," *Bolshaya Sovetskaya Entsyklopediya*, vol. XXXII, column 377.

57. The difference between the extensive herding economy of the nomad and the valued intensive agriculture of the Russian settler is illustrated by the fact that while the latter received an average income of 19 roubles 20 kop. per acre the former received only 2 roubles 73 kop. Safarov, op. cit., p. 45.

than the Kirghiz. In the 1860s the Taranchi and Dungans[58] revolted against the Chinese tyranny and corruption in Sinkiang. The rebellion (1862–1877) was suppressed by the Chinese with great cruelty. In the meantime Russia had occupied the Kulja area to pacify it and keep the revolt from spreading to its native peoples. When the Russians left the country in 1881 in accordance with the terms of the Treaty of St. Petersburg they took some of the Dungans and Taranchi with them, though most had fled earlier into Russian territory. The Dungans lived mostly in Semirechie oblast (14,130 out of a total of 16,279 in Russian Turkistan, according to the Census of 1897).[59]

The great claim of the Russians that the Russian peasants on the land would teach the natives a higher and superior culture must be taken with no little amount of reservation. According to the official report of Count Palen (q.v.)

> Neither in the sense of the variety of culture, nor in the sense of the system of farming have the Russians surpassed the sedentary natives—Taranchi and Dungans; on the contrary, the latter raise rice, olives, different kinds of vegetables, grapes, pears, and even cotton, which demands a much more intensive culture than the usual peasant economy. Even the economy of the Kirghiz nomads, in the sense of adaptation to the natural conditions of the oblast, but naturally not in the sense of technique, stands higher than the economy of the Russians.

The report of Palen goes on to say

> The cultivation of land on the peasant sections is most primitive. They plow to the depth of 2–4 vershoks[60] for one time, more with the spring. Manure is not

58. The Taranchi are a people of mixed Turkic, eastern Iranian, and other mixtures. The origin of the Dungans or Chinese Moslems is still to be settled definitely. Massalsky regards them as Mohammedanized Chinese while other authors think they are Sinized elements of the old Turkic Uighurs. Evkall thinks they are the descendants of Arab mercenaries entering the country from the eighth century A.D. and now much diluted by marriage among the Chinese. See Waldemar Jochelson, *Peoples of Asiatic Russia* (New York, 1928), p. 104; Robert Evkall, *Cultural Relations on the Kansu-Tibetan Frontier* (Chicago, 1939), p. 8; see also Owen Lattimore, *Pivot of Asia; Sinkiang and the Inner Asian Frontiers of China and Russia* (Boston, 1950); Taranchis, p. 126, 196; Dungans, pp. 141, 143.

59. Jochelson, op. cit., p. 105.

60. One vershok = 1.75 inches.

used. The harvest, first reaching up to 150–200 puds per dessiatine[,] is lowered to 30–60 puds on peasant land in constant use.[61]

Such a primitive and inefficient technique of agriculture goes far to explain why the Russian peasant's appetite for nomad land was ever increasing and why they constantly strove to get more, legally or illegally.

The situation would have been bad enough if the lands went only to Russian peasants. Speculation and official corruption were rife in the disposition of these lands. In 1916 General Kuropatkin wrote in his journal:

> Especially inadmissible to me is the giving in 1913, 1914 and 1915 in Semirechie oblast of 1,800,000 dessiatines of *pasture land to various individuals including* 10,000 dessiatines to Porotikov, police chief of the city of Verny. I am afraid that this will be worse than the famous "Baskir land" [scandal]. We ourselves did not know at what we were driving. Turning the Kirghiz to sedentary life we parcelled out among them only the plough lands while the pasture lands—1,800,000 dessiatines—we gave to speculators, not to the Kirghiz. At the same time there took place a bacchanalia in all oblasts of the *krai* with the forest lands of the krai.[62]

In conclusion a few words need be said about the situation among the Turkomans of the Transcaspian region.

The Russians came into this area later than into the other localities of Central Asia, the Turkomans not laying down their arms until after the great siege of Geok Tēpē (1881). Russian colonization here was slight and though the Russians formed 10% of the population in 1914 they were mostly soldiers in garrison. The region is dominated by desert and was the largest and most thinly populated of all the regions of Russian Central Asia. Only the southwest is sufficiently irrigated by the waters of the Murgab and Tedjen rivers. For the rest of this enormous region water was provided only by wells and karez.

The oasis of Merv saw a great extension of cotton growing which already by 1916 constituted 44.6% of the communal sown area, and

61. Quoted in Safarov, op. cit., p. 46.

62. Kuropatkin's Journal, "Vosstanie 1916 g.v Srednei Azii," *Krasnyi Arkhiv* (hereafter cited as K.A.) 3, no. 34 (1929), p. 65. Emphasis in original.

averaged 49.5% of the private mulk lands.[63] General Kuropatkin, visiting the area in 1916, found that some of the Turkomans had prospered greatly from cotton while the rest had become impoverished. Conflict with the Russians in the economic sphere was confined largely to disputes over water, the Russians taking over the water and selling it back to the natives. In the appropriation of water, the Tsarist estate of Bairam-Ali, near Merv, set up to teach the natives improved techniques of agriculture, was especially guilty.

63. Shestakov, op. cit., p. 106.

3

The Political Background to the Revolt of 1916

A. The Administration of the Country

Tsarist Russian Central Asia may be characterized as a military-police state ruled by a viceroy (the Governor-General) who was endowed with very great powers. There were governor-generals in other parts of Russia (Poland, the Caucasus), but none had the wide powers accorded to their Turkistan colleague. General von Kaufman, the first Governor-General of Turkistan (1867–1883) was attended by the pomp and show of a king although his successors preferred to be more modest.

Unlike the rest of Asiatic Russia the Turkistan Governor-Generalship was subject to the War Ministry and not to the Ministry of the Interior. Since the Governor-General was the *alter ego* of the War Ministry and owed his rank of general to it, their views coincided on matters and they ran the country as it pleased them, the Tsar being usually too undecided to take any active part. In this situation not only was the Ministry of the Interior checkmated but also the Ministry of Foreign Affairs. General von Kaufman was given full diplomatic powers to make treaties with the Central Asian khanates while his successors also enjoyed wide powers. As with Ermolev in the Caucasus and later Alexeiev in the Far East these viceroys greatly complicated the conduct of foreign relations by the Ministry of Foreign Affairs.

On the lower level there was the oblast or province governed by a governor, the uezd or district governed by a *nachalnik*, and the *uchast* or sub-division, formed for police purposes, was headed by the *pristav* or police chief. All of these officials were military men, the governor being of general and the nachalnik and pristav of field rank (major or colonel).

In addition to the military administration of the country there were large bodies of troops stationed there. In 1889, after a trip to Russian Central Asia the year previously, Lord Curzon wrote, "Russian Central Asia is indeed one vast camp, and the traveller, who in the course of several weeks' journey scarcely sets eyes upon a Russian civilian, comes away with respect for the discretion, but without much surprise at the peaceful attitude of the people."[1] The presence of large bodies of soldiers excited comment by other travellers. In 1911 the number of Russian soldiers was given as 125,000,[2] even though the danger from the side of the British had passed. The cost of such an occupation was great and only by not including military costs incurred there could the Governor-Generals avoid showing a deficit in the budget for Russian Central Asia.

Only in the fields of Finance, Education, and the Postal and Telegraphic services did the general legislation of the Empire apply. In other departments important deviations were introduced in keeping with the special position of the country. Especially important were the changes in agrarian regulations, justice, and taxation.

The Governor-Generalship of Turkistan with headquarters at Tashkent had at its root the oblasts of Ferghana, Syr Darya, and Samarkand. These were governed on the basis of the Turkistan polozhenie or law code. To the governor-generalship there also belonged Semirechie (which prior to 1897 had been under the Steppe Governor-Generalship) though governed by the Steppe polozhenie and the Transcaspian oblast governed by the Transcaspian provisional polozhenie. The khanates of

1. Curzon, op. cit., p. 386.

2. William L. Curtis, *Turkestan, The Heart of Asia* (New York, 1911), p. 109. Everything was militarized, even the river fleet (the Amu-Darya flotilla) and the railway lines, on which there were stationed military railway battalions.

Khiva and Bukhara stood in a vassal protectorate position to Russia and were not included in the Turkistan Governor-Generalship.

Outside of the Turkistan Governor-Generalship there stood the Steppe oblasts of Akmolinsk, Semipalatinsk, Uralsk, and Turgai, governed, together with Semirechie, on the bases of the Steppe polozhenie. They were subject to the control of the Ministry of the Interior (except Semirechie). A Steppe Governor-General headed the oblasts of Akmolinsk and Semipalatinsk (formerly Semirechie also) and had his headquarters at Omsk. Governors headed the oblasts, with military governors of oblasts in Semirechie and Uralsk. The headquarters of the governments were: the main headquarters for the oblasts of Akmolinsk and Semipalatinsk at Omsk; for the oblasts, Akmolinsk was provisionally at Omsk, Semipalatinsk at the city of Semipalatinsk, Semirechie at Verny, Uralsk at Uralsk, and Turgai at Orenburg. The uezd headquarters were in the cities that bore the name of the uezd.[3]

Steppe Oblasts

Oblasts	*Uezds*
Akmolinsk	Omsk
	Petropavlovsk
	Kokchetavsk
	Akmolinsk
	Atbasarsk
Semirechie	Verny
	Kopal
	Pishpek
	Lepsinsk
	Przhcvalsk
	Jarkent

continued

3. For the administrative setup see *Aziatskaya Rossiya* (St. Petersburg, 1914), vol. I, pp. 54–59.

Steppe Oblasts *continued*

Oblasts	*Uezds*
Semipalatinsk	Semipalatinsk
	Pavlodarsk
	Karkaralinsk
	Ust Kamenogorsk
	Zaisan
Uralsk	Uralsk
	Lbishchensk
	Gurevsk
	Temirsk
Turgai	Aktiubinsk
	Kustanaisk
	Irgizsk
	Turgai

Turkistan Oblasts

Oblasts	*Uezds*
Syr Darya	Amu Darya *otdel* (special division)
	Kazalinsk
	Perovsk
	Chimkent
	Aulie-ata
	Tashkent
Ferghana	Kokand
	Skobelev
	Andijan
	Namangan
	Osh
Samarkand	Samarkand
	Katta Kurgan
	Khojent
	Jizak

The uezd name corresponded with the most important city in the uezd, except for Skobelev uezd where Kokand was much more important than Skobelev city.

Transcaspia oblast Uezd	H.Q. Ashkhabad Headquarters
Ashkhabad	Ashkhabad
Krasnovodsk	Krasnovodsk
Mangishlak	Ft. Alexandrovsk
Tejend	Karrikent
Merv	Merv

Below the *pristatvos* there was a division into village communities, the so-called *aksakalstvo* composed of from 1,000–2,000 households and making up one village. Even the nomads were grouped into village communities, the so-called aul (about 15–20 kibitkas), more auls into a *volost*, which corresponded somewhat to the old tribal division.[4] These units were headed by a native official called *volostnoi, aksakal* (white beard), or, more commonly, *starshina* (elder). In addition there was the native judge called among the Sart population *kazii* and among the nomads *bii*. More influential than the elder among the nomads was the clerk or scribe who was interposed between the natives and the Russian authorities and who used his function of interpreter recklessly. In the Sart towns the houses were divided into sets of 50. From the 50 householders one was chosen to be *Ellik-bashi* or "head of fifty" while over him was a *Ming-bashi* or "head of a thousand," who was responsible to the Russian authorities. The native officials were appointed by the Russian officials, usually the governor, but in 1886 with the promulgation of a new polozhenie these were made elective with confirmation by the Russian authorities. The elder could not be elected more than twice in succession and his term of office was for three years.

4. Essad Sabit, "Die politische Lage in Russisch-Zentralasien," *Deutsche Rundschau*, Band CCII (1925), p. 272.

The best element of the administration of Turkistan were the uezd heads and the pristavs (two to four per uezd). They were military officers with years of service in the army, who often knew well the country and the inhabitants. But there was little scope here for a career. The governors of the provinces were generals sent out by St. Petersburg while there was nothing comparable to the British Indian service in conditions of service. Salaries were poor and no bonus was given for service in a strange country so different from Russia proper. The number of Russian officials was quite inadequate to the needs of the country while their imperfect acquaintance with the native tongue forced them to deal through interpreters who often had their own axes to grind. The service also suffered from the first from the tendency to regard Turkistan as a rehabilitation centre for officers who had fallen from official favor or those whose reputation had become tarnished for one reason or another.

What was the success of the Russian administration among the natives? To answer this question let us first take the Kirghiz and Kazakh nomads.

At the time of the Russian conquest the Kirghiz and Kazakh peoples were divided into *rods*[5] or tribes, the leaders of whom were called among the Kazakhs "sultans" and among the Kirghiz "manaps." The rank was hereditary with the eldest son; the *rod* leader is pictured by a series of authorities (Grodekov, Barthold, Baron Meyendorf, and others) as the active organizer of the life of the *rod*.[6] It was he who organized the migrations, concluded agreements with other *rods* and governments and directed the holding of court. Though he had no personal property he could dispose of the property of the tribe.

The conquest of the Russians changed the position of the manap. Although the volost in the beginning corresponded with the *rod* this

5 The Russian word *rod* is a rather indefinite expression meaning "family," "kin," generation, tribe, clan, blood, stock, etc. Here it may be translated as "tribe," used in the sense of a rather loose and constantly shifting confederation rather than in a strict genealogical sense.

6. Broido, op. cit., p. 414.

was changed so that the volost artfully included two *rods* or more. This was a deliberate attempt by the Russian officials to undermine the authority of the *rod* leader as the peace of the steppe was feared for as long as he preserved his power over the *rod*.[7] The collection of taxes in the volost was concentrated into the hands of the volost head along with the power to impose fines of up to 3 roubles. Control over the collection of these sums was poor especially in view of the nomadic character of the life of the inhabitants.

The new situation brought about a great struggle for election to office among the *rods*. The Russian official was placed in a very advantageous position inasmuch as he could reject the candidature of any nomad aspirant to office. Hence there was competition to secure his favor by means of bribes. The increasing division between the poor and the rich,[8] the displacement of the material economy of the tribe by a trade-money economy and the substitution of the rule of the manap over the *rod* for that of the volost brought a disintegration of the old patriarchal order. Some of the manaps brought their wealth into play to buy office while the others were elbowed out of power.

It is in this setting that we see the workings of the "party" system. The "party system" was in essence the contesting by one manap with another one for the right to hold office. Each gathered around him his adherents or "party."

Elections took place in the following manner. The auls elected the *piatidesyatniki* (representatives of 50) and then the latter elected the volost head. All this took place under the supervision of the uezd nachalnik and with the active participation of his interpreter. Each party had before the election tried to secure a majority. One of the favorite methods used was the registering to the volost of fictitious or temporary kibitkas, the owners of whom were represented as having broken away from another aul. It was the duty of the election overseer to accept these kibitkas as bona fide or to reject them.

7. Galuzo, op. cit., p. 29.

8. By 1910 according to the figures of A. Bukeikhanov the poor section of the Kirghiz population numbered 60.52% while the rich 21.9%. Shestakov, op. cit., p. 96.

Manipulations for the change of auls were carried on long before election time. An example will serve to illustrate the manner in which the system worked. Let us suppose that there are 97 kibitka owners in an aul, having the right to elect two piatidesyatniki with party A having 50 votes and party B, 47. Party A could then elect two representatives while party B would elect none. But if five kibitka owners belonging to party B in a different village petitioned successfully to the uezd nachalnik to be enumerated in the first aul the tables were reversed and party B elected the two representatives. And if there were 25 piatidesyatniki in the volost, with party A having 13 and party B 12, the transferring of the five kibitka owners to party B would have remarkable results. At the elections party A would elect 11 piatidesyatniki while party B would elect 13–14 and thus elect the volost head judges and other volost officials from their party.[9]

It will be readily apparent from the foregoing what a tremendous lever the Russian officials had for making exactions on the winning party through their power to reject candidates, institute investigations, accept or reject petitions for transference of kibitkas, etc.

Sometimes an aspirant would institute a criminal investigation against a rival candidate who seemed capable of winning. The uezd head could either reject the charge or suspend the candidate and institute an investigation.

In some elections there developed a three-cornered fight. If one of the parties doubted its chances of winning it might ally itself with the party that seemed about to win and ready to pay the most. Or, if it feared the majority party, it might ally itself with the other, weaker party.

As soon as the election was over the winning side began to take measures to secure victory in the next contest. Similarly the losing party took steps to win the next election. In trying to turn the favor of the "*nachalstvo*" towards its side no one was overlooked from the uezd head to the last *jigit* or mounted native escort. The expenses of securing an election took on huge dimensions. A candidate might spend

9. See Broido, op. cit., pp. 414–415; Galuzo, op. cit., p. 31.

5,000, 10,000, 20,000, 30,000, and even 40,000 roubles when his future salary for the three-year term of office would not exceed 900–1,500 roubles.[10] The most backward and insignificant volost would call for an expenditure of 2,000–3,000 roubles.

The winning party, after the election, began recouping their election costs and exploiting their privileged position. This was done in various ways. In the first place a multitude of illegal exactions and taxes were levied which were used in part to prepare the way for the future election. The best hay field and pasture lands were presented to party members at the expense of the opposite party. Various duties and services were also levied on members of the opposition party such as: road duties, the requisition of horses for the travel of various officials, the feeding of many officials in the steppe for which the uezd administration usually paid nothing, the presentation of *yurts* (native tents) for the use of administration employees, surveyors, markers, agronomists, botanists, hydrotechnicians, railway men, and others. In the latter case the volost government was paid for the yurts, which meant that the majority party kept the money paid for the yurts of the minority.[11] If the yurts were not given them they were taken and the recalcitrant was packed off to jail for "resistance to the government."

The dominant party used various methods against unsubmissive persons. Physical force and even murder were employed.[12] The people's court was employed; a false criminal proceeding was instituted, the recalcitrant was most commonly found guilty of horse-stealing, and the court decision carried out by the general administration.

When counselled by some people to turn to the Russian authorities the oppressed replied that they would not be allowed to go to the governor while the uezd head would turn them away.[13] Or the complaint

10. Deposition of the engineer Tynyshpaev: *Vosstanie 1916 g.v Kirgizstane*, p. 138.

11. Broido, op. cit., pp. 417–418. The *yurt* is a cylindro-dome-shaped felt tent used by Turkic tribes.

12. Report of the Kashgar Consulate dragoman Stefanovich: *Vosstanie 1916 g.v Kirgizstane*, p. 111.

13. Broido, op. cit., p. 416.

might be "investigated" and quashed, it being declared made "out of party hatred" (a magical phrase in Semirechie).[14]

Under this system the pettiest of officials prospered (*strazhniki* or mounted policemen, translators, etc.). In Semirechie bribe-taking was not the usual crude type but of an organized and hierarchic form. The party leader, in the majority of cases, distributed the rewards through the ranks. In this manner all members of the administration were closely tied to one another and this guaranteed that no complaint would be received or if received that nothing would be found to substantiate the charges inasmuch as to give anyone else away would be to give oneself away.

Among the Sarts there was not such a luxuriant development of the fine art of corruption but here too the incidence of bribe-taking, illegal or excessive exactions, etc. was great. The situation among the Turkomans seems to have been better than in other parts of the *krai*, though information on this point is scanty. General Kuropatkin in 1916 found that while the rest of the krai was dissatisfied with their native judges the Transcaspian oblast was content with theirs.[15]

B. The Political Situation up to 1898

From their first appearance in Central Asia the Russians showed great interest in securing the peace and internal security of the country. One of the most effective means of doing this was by a system of gerrymandered boundaries[16] and the establishment of "native states" (Khiva and Bukhara).[17] The result of this was that no one people was entirely included in a single oblast or native state; each people had different governments to face. Thus the Uzbeks were found in the native states of Khiva and Bukhara and in the oblasts of Samarkand,

14. Ibid., p. 416.

15. Report of A. N. Kuropatkin to Nicholas Romanov, "Vosstanie 1916 g.v Srednei Azii," op. cit., p. 76.

16. The same policy pursued by Chinese *vis-à-vis* the Mongols, see Lattimore's article "Mongolia" in *China Year Book*, 1933, p. 192.

17. For the Chinese policy in creating such "native states" in Sinkiang, see Owen Lattimore, *Pivot of Asia* (Boston, 1950), p. 8.

Syr Darya, and Ferghana; Kazakhs were present in large numbers in Syr Darya and also in Semirechie; the Tajiks occupied portions of the Bukharan khanate and Ferghana oblast; the Kirghiz were present in Ferghana and Semirechie; although most of the Turkomans were in Transcaspia some were also found in the khanate of Khiva. There were also present in Transcaspia Uzbeks, Kazakhs, and Kara-Kalpaks. The division of nationalities rendered any national political combination against the Russians difficult.[18]

Probably the most potent enemy of Russian rule was the Moslem clergy, notably among the sedentary population. The accounts of early travellers like Vambery readily attest to the fierce fanaticism of the Moslems.

General von Kaufman saw Islam as an enemy which might stir up the people to rebellion. To the end of weakening it he undertook a series of measures. He suppressed the post of *kazi-kalyan*[19] as well as that of *reis*, a *custos morum* whose job it was to see that the people followed the rules laid down by the Shariat, and obtained an exception to the law of the empire, under which the authority of the mufti of Ufa (city now in Bashkir Republic of Soviet Union) extended to all oblasts of the Empire, so that it had no force in Turkistan. Later the pilgrimage to Mecca was suppressed for a time, the *zyaket* tax[20] was removed and the further endowment of *vakuf* land was allowed only with the permission of the governor, which was rarely given.

Despite the measures that von Kaufman took which earned him the hatred of the clergy, he left much undone in the way of controlling Islam. He felt that Moslem culture was doomed to disappear and that if left to itself it would die a natural death.[21] While he did not leave the spiritual life of the natives completely alone he apparently subjected

18. William Mandel, *The Soviet Far East and Central Asia* (New York, 1944), pp. 100–101.

19. *Kazi-kalyan*—a superior Moslem spiritual authority.

20. *Zyaket*—a religious tax levied by Moslem law on land, cattle, the product of trade, etc.

21. Barthold, op. cit., p. 284.

it to a weak supervision. His successors went even further and completely neglected the religious life of the natives: the schools, clergy, and religious orders were left without any kind of supervision by the government.

The contact of the native masses with the Russian official was even more lessened by the new polozhenie of 1886. The number of Russian uezd officials before 1886 was insufficient but the new polozhenie decreased the number to a dangerous low. It is sufficient to point out that the Ferghana oblast with 1.5 million people was reduced, in the number of uezd heads, their assistants, and the uezd police inspectors, to only 17 persons while the Elizavetpol *gubernia*[22] in Russia proper, similar to it in the composition of its population and with 800,000 persons, had 43; moreover the duties of the latter were much less complicated.[23]

In addition the polozhenie took the appointment of native volost officials out of the hands of the Russian officials and made them elective while there was also effected a separation of the judiciary and the administration. The Russian official was stripped of the power to look after the general welfare of the people and became exclusively a military-police official.

The spirit of opposition to Russian rule was expressed most vigorously in Ferghana oblast (the former Kokand khanate) the most economically developed oblast of the krai. From the time of its conquest until 1885 there hardly went by a year that some band of mutineers or brigands did not wander about Ferghana. In the 1870s there occurred the uprising of Pulatkhan seizing almost the whole Ferghana oblast. In the 1880s we come to the period of the "pseudo-khans," called such because the leaders of the robber bands represented themselves as heirs of the deposed khan of Kokand. These leaders found ready material at hand in the many former officials, soldiers, and servants of the former

22. "The Russian name for province is *Guberniya* (Government) or *Oblast* (Territory). . . . Those called *Guberniya* were of greater importance, both numerically and economically." Jochelson, op. cit., p. 13.

23. Report of Lt. Gen. Korolkov to Gov. Gen. Dukhovsky, Aug. 3, 1898: "Andizhanskoe vosstanie 1898 g.," K.A. 1, no. 86 (1938), p. 158.

khan, out of a job and ready to listen to the appeal of any fanatic or robber. The Russian administration attached no political significance to these bands as they robbed the native population as well as the Russians.[24] The Russian authorities were forewarned of every revolt in preparation. The movement of the "pseudo khans" in the early 1880s was broken and fifty leaders were caught by the administration, five of whom were hanged.

In 1885 during the period of Anglo-Russian tension and the Pendjeh incident between the forces of Afghanistan and Russia, a wave of agitation spread over Turkistan and reached Ferghana oblast. Confused rumors were circulated about an imminent war between Russia on one side and Afghanistan and China on the other and of the appearance of a "Mahdi" or Moslem messiah, while announcements were circulated about an imminent Jihad or holy war against the Russians. Again there appeared bands of "pseudo-khans" making raids upon the *kishlak* or Sart village, on the homes of *beks* and volost heads and even taking Tsarist officials as hostages. The leader of the movement was a certain Dervish-khan—Tyura by name—reportedly counting on a general uprising of the people of Ferghana. Though an expedition was dispatched and the bands broken up, Dervish-khan was not caught.

The composition of these bands may be gathered from the following quotation. Writing of captives taken from a unit of Dervish-khan in 1885, General Medinsky stated, "Those of the participants arrested after the disorders, more than 60 persons, presented a pitiful sight, the majority being without homes."[25] Also represented were the poor dekhans, sharecroppers, landless, and homeless wanderers. The great displacement and impoverishment caused by King cotton in Ferghana, the leading cotton oblast, is apparent.

The incidence of robber-band activity did not diminish and it is with this background that we approach the Andijan uprising of 1898.

24. Report of Maj. Gen. Medinsky to Lt. Gen. Kuropatkin, ibid., p. 136.
25. Foreword by E. Steinberg: ibid., p. 125.

C. The Andijan Uprising

On the night of May 17, 1898, there gathered a crowd in the kishlak of Ming-tyube, Margelan uezd of the Ferghana oblast, composed of Kirghiz and Kipchaks from the Osh and Andijan uezds and many local Sart dekhans. They were responding to the declaration of a *gazavat* or holy war against the unbeliever proclaimed by one of the most popular *ishans*[26] of Turkistan, Mahomet-Ali-Khalfa, better known as Madali. After forming these people into units, inflamed by his fanaticism Madali started out for Andijan, horsemen in front and the rest of the mass in the rear. How many people were included in this band is not clear, though according to some sources there were 1,500 persons with Madali. Reaching Andijan at about three o'clock in the morning, the insurgents fell on the barracks of the 20th battalion. The attack was made in complete silence and was totally unexpected by the soldiers. The natives surrounded the camp and set about killing the sleeping soldiers. Part of the soldiers, however, managed to awaken and take arms and under the direction of a Lieutenant Karzeladze rushed at the natives with bayonets and fired shots at the natives who were not armed with firearms. This appeared sufficient to repulse the attackers, who fled. According to the account of witnesses the whole affair took about 15 minutes from the beginning of the attack to the rout of the mutineers. The Russians suffered casualties of 22 soldiers killed and 16 wounded. The attackers were not pursued as the Russian soldiers ran out of ammunition and furthermore had no cavalry force. This was both the beginning and the end of the Andijan uprising. It was not followed by any battles between insurgents and

26. *Ishan*. As used in Turkistan the word means *shaikh*, *murshid*, *pir*, teacher, or guide, in distinction to *murid*, adherent, pupil. The origin of the word is still obscure though it was used in the Middle Ages. The rank of ishan is frequently handed down from father to son. The ishan usually lives, together with his followers, in a monastery or sometimes in the tomb of a saint from which at times he issues forth into the steppes to work among the Kirghiz from whom he receives more substantial presents than from the Sarts. See *Encyclopaedia of Islam* (Leyden and London, 1927), vol. II, p. 533. See also Prince V. Masalsky, *Turkestansky krai* (St. Petersburg, 1913), p. 355 et seq.; Franz von Schwarz, *Turkestan, die Wiege der indogermanischen Völker* (Freiburg im Breisgau, 1900), p. 198.

the government, sieges of cities, or partisan activity usually associated with revolts.

At first glance the whole affair seems to be quite insignificant, and worth only mention in passing. In actuality the Andijan uprising was one of the most important moments in the Tsarist rule of Russian Central Asia. It revealed a widespread dissatisfaction with Russian rule on the part of the natives and a plot to revolt that embraced a significant portion of Turkistan. It is necessary to mention that the insurgents were supported by the people of Andijan, that when they approached the city they were joined by 200 Andijanians. But much more important, it was revealed that not only were the Andijan and Margelan uezds involved in the movement but also all Ferghana, present-day Kirghizia, and in part even Samarkand oblast. According to the plan the Andijan operation of Madali was to take place at the same time as attacks by other parties of insurgents on Osh and Margelan. These other operations were, however, betrayed to the Russian authorities in time for them to take suitable action. Thus the Osh attack never took place, because on May 17 the volost head Karabek Khasanov told the uezd head about the preparations. The leader of the rebels, Umarbek Datkhi was arrested and other precautions were taken. The extent and nature of the plot were discovered only slowly and then only incompletely. Thus General Kuropatkin, the Minister of War, reported to St. Petersburg that "the discovery of this organization and the degree of participation in it of other localities in the region comprises not an easy task in view of the existing means for its fulfilment, facts only now are beginning to fall into our hands."[27]

Part of the significance of the Andijan uprising lies in the fact that it was an attack not on the "peaceful inhabitants" of Central Asia, the officials of the administration or Russian colonists—which would not have been new—but was an open attack upon a Tsarist military garrison. The leaders of the rebellion counted upon the support of the people in a real rebellion against the Russians, not a futile action of

27. Ibid., p. 128.

protest or a predatory act. Its political nature was recognized by the Russians and a very great interest was shown in its suppression and investigation by the highest authorities—General Kuropatkin and Nicholas II.

In its economic motivation the uprising was a measure of the despair of the poor over the cotton crisis which had seized Ferghana in 1897 and 1898 as a consequence of the fall of world cotton prices. The situation may be seen by the following table.[28]

Years	Prices of cotton compared with 1900, taken at 100	Area under cotton in Ferghana in dessiatines
1895	88	109,701
1896	78	128,726
1897	60	116,802
1898	54	106,230

The years of crisis sharply worsened the position of the peasantry and brought them to the side of the ishan. Thus there was represented in the social composition of the revolters not only the clergy, former officers of the Kokand khanate, half-settled Kirghiz and Kipchaks, but a goodly number of Uzbek dekhans or peasants and, to use the expression of the military procurator, a "motley rabble" of day laborers, small traders, "wandering folk, not having a definite calling, and having nothing to lose."

But though the peasants had great economic grievances the leading part was played by religious fanaticism. In reading the depositions made by the leading participants after the revolt one is struck by the fact that nowhere are economic grievances mentioned. When Madali was asked by the Russians why he had revolted he replied:

1. That after the conquest by the Russians there took place a strong deterioration in the morals of the people.
2. The non-compliance with the demands of the Shariat.

28. Galuzo, op. cit., p. 46.

3. That the Russian government though lenient in their relations with the natives forbade pilgrimages to Mecca.
4. That they abolished the zyaket or religious tax.
5. The tampering with vakuf laws.
6. That they did not trouble about the support of morality and family life.[29]

The polozhenie of 1886 had laid a land tax upon vakuf land to which it had not been previously subjected and took from its control some landed areas, thus depriving the clergy of much revenue. The deterioration in morals, noticed by many Western travellers,[30] involved the Moslem youth and alienated them from the clergy. Madali felt deeply about this and ascribed the fall of the Kokand khanate to the fall in morality; the coming of the Russians had made matters much worse. Gambling, drunkenness, and prostitution became synonymous with Russian rule. The abolition of the office of reis greatly loosened the hold of the Moslem clergy on the common people.

Madali was apparently sincerely convinced that his great mission in life was to turn the people from the fleshpots and back to the strict morality of some past age. While still a youth he had made a pilgrimage to Mecca and while there reportedly had visions in which his future role was announced. After his return to Turkistan he soon attracted many followers to his side by his asceticism and sanctity. In addition he acted as a physician to the sick. The many Sufis[31] and pupils who attended him constantly told of his magical powers. Thus it was said that he cooked pilau[32] without a fire.

The fame and power of the ishan grew to such proportions that in 1895 he appointed reis in the localities near Ming-tyube (despite the abolition of the office by the Russians). As in khanate times they were

29. V. P. Salkov, *Andizhanskoe vosstanie 1898 g.* (Kazan, 1901), pp. 79–81.

30. See *inter alia* Curzon, op. cit., p. 399; Woiekof, op. cit., p. 335

31. *Sufi*—follower of a mystical cult of Islam. Present in all Moslem countries but especially in Iran and Central Asia. Sufism taught a renunciation of the material world, seclusion, and a mystical perception of God's truth.

32. *Pilau*—a native dish of steamed rice, vegetables, and mutton.

armed with whips and went about chasing the people to the mosques and beating them for non-fulfillment of the demands of the Shariat. In addition Madali sent a letter to Abdul Hamid, the Turkish Sultan, telling of the deterioration of the moral and religious fiber of the people and of the great need to reform this parlous state of affairs. This was written by one of his followers as Madali himself was illiterate. In answer to this letter he received what purported to be a firman or moral decree from the Sultan of Turkey (in his capacity of Khalif of Islam) as well as an old khalat or robe from the shoulders of the Sultan. Madali firmly believed that both were sent by the Sultan and he became exalted both in his own eyes and in the eyes of the people and believed, probably, that he was called upon to save the people from the Russians. Both the letter and the khalat were forwarded to him by a certain Hadji Abdu-Jalil Mir-Sadyh Karyev.[33] To the letter from

33. The Russian authorities believed that if the plot and the announcement of the gazavat was not conceived in connection with the appearance of Abdu-Jalil in Ferghana, then his presence contributed significantly to its further development (see Report of General Dolinsky to General Dukhovsky: "Andizhanskoe vosstanie 1898 g." K.A. 1, no. 86 [1938], p. 169). Abdu-Jalil was an Andijanian by birth but in early youth made the pilgrimage to Mecca, remaining abroad many years. In 1895 he returned to Turkistan from Constantinople, where he had lived at a Dervish monastery, by the route of India, Yarkand, Khotan, Kashgar, and Kulja, in Sinkiang, penetrating into the Samarkand oblast. He visited Tashkent and finally in the winter of 1895–1896 appeared in Andijan. Rumors were quickly circulated that he brought a hair from the beard of the Prophet.

Hearing that the Andijan authorities were investigating his actions he went to the Margelan uezd where he lived for some time in the villages of Kuva and Sharikhan. Then he disappeared, presumably returning to Turkey.

Abdu-Jalil reappeared in the Samarkand oblast in the winter of 1897–1898, visited Kokand, Margelan, Kuva, and then settled again in the village of Sharikhan. Soon anonymous letters appeared in Kokand asking the rich people to prepare for a gazavat (holy war) and a zyaket (Moslem religious tax) and *kheradzh* (tax on goods in former Kokand khanate) for the last 15 years.

Before the *Uraza** he visited Madali presenting him with the letter from the Sultan and the Sultan's khalat and exhorted him to begin a gazavat against the Russians.

During the attack on Andijan he remained at Sharikhan. With its failure he fled to Kashgar, in Chinese territory in Sinkiang.

**Uraza*—Moslem fast in the month of Ramadan, the ninth month of the Moslem calendar. The fast lasts a whole month, though fasting takes place only in the day time. With evening the fast is ended, and the holiday and celebration begins, often lasting all night.

the Sultan there was affixed a royal seal. The document testifies, in its beginning, to the fact that Madali is a true ishan and ends with an impersonal exhortation to fulfill loyally and sincerely the teachings of Mohammed and to prove this by deeds.

What was the part played by Turkish Pan-Islamism in this movement is difficult to determine.[34] The firman was almost certainly a forgery. Both the paper and the handwriting were Turkistani while it is extremely doubtful that the Sultan would have bothered himself personally with such an insignificant personage as the Madali. But that Abdu-Jalil was acting as a Turkish agent is probably true, though we have no precise information on this score. In his struggle to blow life into the fey Ottoman Empire and secure it against the further encroachments of the Western Powers[35] Abdul Hamid made great use of the Pan-Islamic movement initiated in the reign of his predecessor Abdul Azziz and the revival of the Caliphate in the person of the Turkish Sultan. To counter machinations of the Russians in Armenia and the Balkans Abdul Hamid sent his agents into Afghanistan, Central Asia, the Trans-Volga, the Caucasus, etc. It is in this background that there appeared in Peshawar in 1885 a certain Abdul-Kerimbek scattering proclamations calling for a holy war and the exchange of accredited envoys between Afghanistan and Turkey. He adopted the title of "Defender of the faith," began to mint money to finance a Holy War, and had printed in Kabul two books on the Jihad under his direction.

The Tsarist government showed great interest in the question of Pan-Islamic connections with the Andijan affair. In reading the report of General Kuropatkin about the uprising the Tsar underscored the lines telling of the Sultan's letter, and later the Russian ambassador

34. The entire problem of the origins, aims, and influence of Pan-Islamism, in its present state of study, is ridden with contradictory views, obfuscation, and general lack of information. On this see the important article by Dwight E. Lee, "The Origins of Pan-Islamism," *American Historical Review*, vol. XLVII (1941), pp. 278–287.

35. Pan-Islamism was used even more by Abdul Hamid and by the conservative force of the entire Moslem religion to oppose at home the innovationists of European notions of nationalism, freedom, and democracy. H. Kohn, *History of Nationalism in the East* (New York, 1929), p. 51.

in Constantinople was instructed by St. Petersburg to find out if the Sultan actually wrote the letter. Possibly it was more pleasing to the Tsarist ego to explain the revolt as the result of Pan-Islamic instigation rather than in terms of native dissatisfaction with Tsarist exploitation and corruption.

The revolt was led by the clergy and feudal remnants. What was the role of the other classes? Though the ishan announced on several occasions before the rebellion that members of the well-to-do element were on the side of the people and had affixed their seals to the pact calling for a holy war, in actuality only 12 such persons signed the pact and this class was in general opposed to the rebellion. They feared the Russian power and they were in a much better position due to their better education, contacts with Russians, official and commercial, to know the real struggle of the two opponents. After the rebellion they vied with each other in expressing their loyalty and devotion to the Russian administration. Thus the Tashkent "influential natives"[36] expressed "their very loyal feeling and their dissatisfaction in relation to the wicked attack on Andijan, and asked permission to collect among themselves a sum for the families of the lower ranks who were killed." In his trip through Samarkand, Katta Kurgan, and other places the new Governor-General, General Dukhovsky, heard similar sentiments expressed by deputations of these influential persons.[37]

The common people believed in the holiness of the ishan and were not in as good a position to know the real strength of Russian arms. The locality was an isolated one and contact with Russians was limited. Russian rule was thought of as accidental, transitory, unnecessary, and needlessly burdensome. In addition there had been a decrease in recent times in the number of troops stationed in Ferghana. There were only two companies of soldiers in Andijan and moreover, it being May,

36. The term "respectable natives" (*pochetonye lits*) occurs again and again in Russian official documents and refers to the well-to-do, prominent members of the community as opposed to the common people.

37. For this situation of part of the old ruling class identifying itself with the new Russian ruling class, see Owen Lattimore, *Situation in Asia* (Boston, 1949), p. 16.

the Cossack and artillery horses were out to pasture far from the barracks.

The native volost officials proved to be a great disappointment to the Russians. Instead of actively helping the government they were at best passive spectators while there was one case (the Kulinsky volost head) of active help to the ishan. Though they must have known of the preparations only one (the Ming-tyubinsk volost head) reported it to the Russian authorities and then only on the eve of the attack though he admitted he knew of the plot on May 13.

Punishment was meted out not only to the actual participants in the revolt but to all who were involved in any way in its preparation. The first measure was the general flogging with *nagaikas* or Cossack whips of those arrested on orders of General Povalo-Shveikovsky, the former Governor-General. Concerning this flogging he reported to St. Petersburg that this "created a splendid impression both on the native population and on the army" though General Korolkov who was to make an official enquiry into the causes of the revolt was to admit later that the prison hospitals were filled to overflow from the effects of this measure.

Over 400 persons were convicted, 18 of whom were hanged including the Madali and his nephew whom he had named to occupy the throne of Kokand. The rest received sentences of penal servitude and banishment. The guilty villages of Ming-tyube and Haukata were razed to the ground, the inhabitants ejected and the ground seized for the settling of Russian colonies. A fine of 300,000 roubles was levied on the inhabitants of Ferghana oblast.

The Russian authorities attributed the revolt to Moslem fanaticism and the "liberalism" of the polozhenie of 1886. They called for its repeal and a return to the *status quo ante*. General Kuropatkin,[38]

38. *Alexander Nicholas Kuropatkin* (1848–1921). Entered army in 1864. Participated in the conquest of Samarkand and Kokand, and in the Kulja operation. Greatly distinguished himself in the Russo-Turkish war of 1877–1878 where he served as chief of staff to the younger Skobelev. His book on the war—*Lovcha and Plevna* (1885) is still the classic work on the subject. After the war he commanded the Turkistan Rifle Brigade and

probably the most enlightened and best informed administrator of Russian Central Asia, in his report to Nicholas II reported the following recommendations made by General Korolkov: higher salaries for the officials, more officials, 48 instead of 18 uchast pristavs, increasing the military forces in Ferghana, the strengthening of the Russian element, the control by officials of Moslem religious life, the provision of dispensaries especially for Moslem women, persuading the Orthodox Church to exercise more cultural influence over the natives, the giving to the Governor-General of the right to banish ishans and undesirables, not allowing Moslems to head uezds and uchasts, increasing the opportunities offered native youths upon graduation from Russian or city schools, giving officials more jurisdiction over Moslem daily life, and finally certain administrative reforms.[39]

Though perhaps a seemingly inordinate amount of attention has been devoted in these pages to the Andijan uprising, it is justified by the very intimate connection between this uprising and the events among the Sarts in the Revolt of 1916. As we shall later see there is a close parallel between the two revolts, 1898 and 1916, in the nature

---

enhanced his fame still further by taking part in a march of 500 miles from Tashkent to Geok-Tēpē, where he participated in the storming of the latter place which closed the campaign against the Turkomans. In 1882 he was promoted to the rank of major general and was generally regarded by the army as natural successor to Skobelev. From 1890 to 1898 he served as Governor-General of Turkistan and from 1898 to 1904 as Minister of War. In the Russo-Japanese War he was given command of all forces. The Japanese forces inflicted a series of defeats on Kuropatkin, who nevertheless managed to pull his forces northward to Mukden in skilfully executed retreats. The rout of the Russian forces at Mukden caused Kuropatkin to resign his command to Gen. Linievich after which he commanded one of the three armies in Manchuria. Kuropatkin's failure may be explained partly by the meddlesome interference of Admiral Alexeiev, the viceroy of Russia's Far East possessions, and by Kuropatkin's own mistakes—mistakes which he admitted himself in his account of the war (*The Russian Army and the Japanese War*, 1909).

Kuropatkin commanded an army during World War I until July 1916, when he was appointed Turkistan Governor-General. In April 1917, he was ousted from his position after the overthrow of the Tsarist government. Later in the year he appears teaching in a village school. He died in Shemshurino (Pskov) in February 1921.

39. Report of Kuropatkin to Nicholas II: "Andizhanskoe vosstanie 1898 g.," K.A. 1, no. 86 (1938), pp. 175–178.

of class participation, the leadership, the suppression, and the recommendations made. In his recommendations and the justification of his actions after the Revolt of 1916 General Kuropatkin, who was a leader in suppressing both affairs, cited directly the actions taken during the Andijan affair as a precedent guiding his actions.[40]

D. The Political Situation after 1898

1. Enquiry of Count Palen

In examining the scene after the uprising of 1898 one is immediately struck by the impression that, though the Tsarist authorities were given quite a start by this incident, little was done beyond severe punishment of the rebels and the strengthening of forces in the country. The Russian element was strengthened and the Russian population was provided with military rifles. This armament had begun in the early 1890s but after the Andijan uprising and especially after the Boxer Rebellion in China it was expanded to a general armament (one rifle per family).

How little the causes of discontent had been removed was shockingly demonstrated by the official enquiry of Senator Count Palen made in 1906. The graft, corruption, land-grabbing, etc. that had been decried in the earliest days of the Russian conquest were found to have become much worse in recent years. The report of Count Palen shook the confidence of the country in the Turkistan administration. After 1906 the question of an over-hauling of the entire structure received much attention, but the Revolt of 1916 found the reforms still waiting to be put into effect.

2. The Political Situation among the Sarts

The first stirrings of a political revolutionary opposition in Russian Turkistan were found not among the natives but among the Russians resident there. In the period 1905–1907 there developed among them a few feeble responses to the great events of the 1905 Revolution

40. K.A. 3, no. 34 (1929), pp. 86–87.

taking place in Russia. There was a "movement" among the liberal official-intelligentsia class, demonstrations with red flags, soldier uprisings (Tashkent, Ashkhabad, Kushka), and railway strikes. But there was no connection between these manifestations and the great native mass of the population. This movement was regarded by the liberal lawyers, engineers, doctors, and officials as solely the affair "of the Russian progressive community."[41] The Russian soldiers and workmen were attracted to the SR party.[42] The "SDs," or Social Democrats, the future Bolsheviks, were very weakly represented although they succeeded in 1907 in electing the former vice-governor Nalivkin to the 2nd State Duma.

Traces of Pan-Islamism in Russian Central Asia have already been remarked before and during the Andijan affair and these were to be strengthened during the years ahead. In opposition to it there grew up among the Sarts a progressive nationalist movement, the followers of whom were known as Jadids (literally adherents of the new method). This was fostered by a number of factors: the increasing number of Sarts going to Russia for study and travel and their contact with progressive Russian opinion, the decreased fanaticism of the natives,[43] and contact, though limited, with other progressive movements in the Islamic world. Abdul Hamid had unwittingly aided the development of such progressive tendencies when he had set the minds of the Moslem peoples back to the time when they were all united and at the zenith of their power. Research by Moslem scholars was beginning to show that greater freedom of religious thought coincided with the halcyon days

41. Safarov, op. cit., p. 53.

42. Social Revolutionary Party. See footnote 52.

43. The Syr Darya oblast governor in 1909 made the following statement: "During the last half century the position of the ishans in society has changed significantly. Before the people bore themselves with superstitious fear towards representatives of the ishan class. One may say with certainty that by this time the religious fanaticism of the natives has weakened in a significant measure in the sense of intolerance towards . . . foreigners. The ishans themselves do not always manifest the moral qualities indispensable for religious leadership of the Sarts and the people have noticed this." Quoted by Galuzo, op. cit., p. 144.

of the Islamic world. Moreover the stimulus of Pan-Islamism showed that reforms would have to be made if Islam were to effectively resist the advances of Europe.[44]

The Jadids represented the left wing of Pan-Islamism in Russian Central Asia. They came from the ranks of petty and middle traders and the intellectual class with occasional support from the great merchants.

The Jadids were represented by two organizations, the "Young Party" located at Kokand with about 50 members in its ranks in 1912 and the group located around Old Tashkent. In each group there was a radical and a moderate faction. The differences between the two may be summed up by quoting a report of the Okhrana or Secret Police.

> The Pan-Islamists / the Jadids / are divided into two factions, often hostile towards each other, one of these, the more numerous and composed of influential persons, occupies in society a more or less influential position—teachers, mullahs, lawyers, merchants. In its political outlook it differs little from the Constitutional Democratic Party. The other faction is very few in number (Mlado-Tatari) and recruited from the youth (clerks, shop salesmen, and in part, teachers) and adheres to the program and tactics of the Social-Revolutionaries).[45]

The comparison of the Mlado Tatar (Young Tatar) Jadids with the "SRs" shows the presence of a group favoring a revolutionary outburst against the Russians to liquidate their rule. Thus in 1908 one of this group, Abdu-Vakhit-Kariev, issued a manifesto calling all Moslems to arms and for a general rising "against the accursed Russians."

Be that as it may the main group of Jadids was much more moderate in its aims. This group had no political platform in the usual sense. Its basic demands were for the establishment of new method schools, the introduction of a new orthography, the elimination of the Arabic-Persian scholars, and the propagation and development of national culture.

This national cultural movement begins with the year 1905. The Jadids plumped hard for the introduction of new schools and inasmuch

44. H. Kohn, op. cit., pp. 51–52.
45. Galuzo, op. cit., p. 145.

as this represents their basic activity some idea of their success may be served by considering the number of schools they opened.[46]

Places schools opened	Number	Year of statistics
Tashkent (city)	12	1912
Turkistan (city)	2	1912
Semirechie oblast	17	1912
Kokand uezd	13	1913
Perovsk uezd	1	1912
Samarkand (city)	2	1911
Bukhara (city)	5	1911
Andijan uezd	3	1912
Total	55	

Thus in seven years the Jadids opened 55 new method schools. This number testifies rather to the insignificance of their practical accomplishments than to their success. However, in spite of small numbers the result was important as it brought the creation of a secular (and increasingly anti-clerical) intelligentsia.

The Right Wing of Pan-Islamism was represented by the Ulema or Moslem Bookmen, the upholders of the old traditions. This movement was made up of the clergy, gentry, and great merchants. While the Jadids centred themselves in the area of the greatest economic development, around Kokand, the Ulema was centred at Bukhara where there was found the greatest concentration of gentry, clergy, and Moslem scholars. While the Jadids were confined to Bukhara, Tashkent, and Kokand the Ulema was represented in all the cities of Central Asia.

Though both groups had as their goal the union of all Moslems a bitter struggle ensued. The Ulema greatly objected to the neglect by the Jadids of the rules of the Shariat, their wearing of European clothes, shaving off their beards, and letting the hair grow on their

46. Ibid., p. 147.

heads. They called the movement "treachery to Islam" and attacked the "Godless" Europeanization.[47]

The year 1905 also saw the appearance of a series of local newspapers. There had already appeared in Turkistan at the turn of the century the Crimean paper *Tardzhiman* ("The Interpreter") edited by the well-known Ismail Gasprinsky calling for a Moslem Turkic cultural revival. These newspapers were published in the native tongues while five or six years before the Bolshevik Revolution there appeared in Russian the progressive *Golos Turkestana*, or "Voice of Turkistan."

The effects of this cultural, political, and nationalist activity were very limited. Except that, because of their impotence when acting alone, many became disposed later to go over to the Bolsheviks. They were confined to the cities and even there only to the small intellectual élite. The Pan-Islamists appealed more to Allah than to the population with their talk of a gazavat or holy war. The illiterate artisans, proletariat, and dekhans continued their labors and ways consecrated by millennial torpor.

3. The Political Situation among the Kazakhs and Kirghiz

The development of political organization and agitation among the Kirghiz and Kazakhs took place very slowly and in a very weak form. The leading reasons for this were: the small numbers living in the cities[48] where political organization is always more easy to begin, and the illiteracy,[49] lack of school facilities, and remoteness and seclusion of many of the nomad areas. Until 1912 there was not one newspaper, and no books, in Kirghiz or Kazakh. Broido, speaking of his experiences in Semirechie, writes: "I never chanced to come upon a single, even rich, yurt [nomad felt tent] where the dwellers knew Moslem writing well, or to find any sort of book and very rarely even the Koran."[50] In view of this it is understandable why the nomads took

47. Safarov, op. cit., p. 54; Galuzo, op. cit., p. 151.
48. In 1920 only 1.3% of the Kirghiz of the Kirghiz SSR were city dwellers.
49. 1.7–4.9% literacy according to gubernia.
50. Broido, op. cit., p. 421.

no part in the great events of 1905; but, it should be remarked, it is equally understandable that when the nomads were directly affected, as in 1916, they reacted in a vigorous return to their ancestral tradition of violence and raiding warfare.

The first signs of political life in the steppes were connected with the Manifesto of 18 February 1905 concerning the calling of a Duma and the Ukaz of 17 April concerning toleration. These acts led to the first political meetings among the nomads which were occupied greatly with the religious and agrarian questions. The discussions led to the separation of two main factions, one religious, Pan-Islamist and Eastern in orientation, the other Western turning towards the Russian intelligentsia and culture. The first was led by the clergy, the second by the intelligentsia. By 1906 the intelligentsia had clarified its political thinking further and there was a gravitation towards the Cadet[51] Party in general though others were attracted to the SDs and SRs.[52] All this, however, was to be submerged by the Stolypin program of reaction after 1907.

The struggle was thereafter carried on by writers and agitators from among the intelligentsia and the growing youth closely affiliated with the Cadet Party. The year 1912 marks an important milestone—the founding of the paper *Kazak* by a group headed by Baitursunov, Bukeikhanov, Dulatov, and others. This group on the one hand struck

51. The Cadets or Constitutional Democrats were a group made up of liberal capitalists, professional people, and landowners. They called for the setting up in Russia of a bourgeois republic or a constitutional monarchy as in Great Britain.

52. The "SRs," or Social Revolutionary Party concentrated their attention on the peasantry and became the revolutionary party *par excellence* of the latter. Their socialism consisted mainly in demanding that all land should belong to the peasants. The SRs were distinguished from the SDs or Social Democrats (made up of Bolshevik and Menshevik wings) in a number of ways. The SRs concentrated their attention on the peasantry while the SDs concentrated on the small industrial proletariat class. The appeal of the SRs was wider, their organization was looser, and they were less hampered by instructions from the centre than the SDs. The SDs had close ties with Western European Socialism and their patriotism was that of the working class of the world. The SRs were distinctly Russian in flavor, outlook, and patriotism. The SRs were inclined to advocate terrorism while the SD leaders roundly condemned this.

out at the intelligentsia for having lost contact with the common folk and for its predilection for office and rank, while on the other hand it attacked Pan-Islamism. Other goals were the placing of military duty among the Kirghiz and Kazakhs on the same basis as that enjoyed by the Cossacks, instruction in schools, and transition to a sedentary life. The Russification policy of the government was attacked, as was its policy of squeezing out the nomad from the land.[53]

The subsequent period up to 1916 may be summarized as witnessing the wider participation and organization of the intelligentsia, the students, and youth in general for promotion of the national and cultural aspirations of the people. Illegal and legal groups were formed among the students, especially, at Omsk, which was the great centre of education. Among the intellectuals there appear individuals and groups dissatisfied with the line taken by the *Kazak* and its directors. They objected to the tie of these persons with the Cadets, their conciliatory line with the Russian officialdom, their appeals to patriotism, and for the participation of the Kirghiz and Kazakhs in military service. There was formed in Tashkent in 1912 the paper *Ushzkuz* which carried on a controversy with the *Kazak*. Its adherents appeared in Semipalatinsk, Omsk, and other places. In 1916 this group took on a socialist tinge.[54]

Thus on the eve of the 1916 uprising there was a thin scattering of intellectuals and students among the nomads agitating for political goals. Though the clergy played some part in these proceedings their influence was much more modest than among the Sarts. There was not and could not be any tie in political development between the nomad and sedentary peoples inasmuch as the Uzbek appeared as a usurer and oppressor among the nomads. Each people was to go its own way in the struggle to come. Islam was, in any case, less organized and more informal among nomads. Islam among settled Central Asians was fortified by considerable property holding. Among the nomads there was no strong property or institutional base.

53. Z. Mindlin, "Kirgizy i revolyutsia," *Novy Vostok*, vol. V (1924), p. 219.
54. Ibid., p. 220.

4

The Revolt of 1916: First Phase

A. War Comes to Turkistan

The outbreak of the first World War reacted unfavorably on the position of the colonies of the European powers in two ways. On the one hand the colony saw suspended all benefits which it had received in the form of European goods, technical know-how, and capital investment while on the other it was required to contribute manpower and great stocks of raw materials and other goods for the war needs of the mother country.

Although the peoples of Russian Central Asia in the first two years of the war were not required to serve in the armed forces or to contribute a labor force for work in Russia, they made heavy contributions to the war effort. The extent of this may be realized from the following statistics (figures of General Kuropatkin) on matériel sent to Russia.

Cotton	40,899,244 puds (1 pud = 36.11 lbs.)
Felt	38,004 sq. arshins (1 arshin = 28 inches)
Cotton seed oil	3,109,000 puds
Soap	229,000 puds
Dressed meat	300,000 puds
Fish	473,928 puds
Castor oil plant (Palma Christi)	50,000 puds

continued

Horses	70,000
Camels	12,797
Carts	270
Yurts	13,441 units

In addition 2.4 million roubles were contributed to the needs of the war.[1]

The demand for "donations" from the natives introduced a further source of malpractice, especially among the Kazakhs and Kirghiz. The demand for greater taxes and for contributions for the war effort enabled the administration to make further demands on the population. There were volost officials that took two to three times as much as they were asked by Petrograd to take, and if the government paid for the articles sent by the nomads these sums were kept by the volost authorities for themselves.[2] The Kirghiz paid 1–3 roubles per yurt for the benefit of the Red Cross, but though there were 40,000 yurts (households) in the Pishpek uezd there was officially reported collected only 2,000 roubles.[3] Other "contributions" were levied for the benefit of the Damskaya Kresta and other charitable societies. Large quantities of yurts (tents) were collected for the war effort, often without recompense, and often these yurts were transported by the nomads to the railway gratis. Individual localities made separate contributions. Thus the village of Novo Nikolaievsk gave 90 horses. The nomads were also asked to provide hospitality without pay to units passing through the steppe.

The Kirghiz and Kazakh nomads fared much worse than the Sarts in one respect—in addition to special taxes and contributions they were required to furnish laborers to work the farms of Russians away at the front. The inhabitants of the three basic oblasts of Turkistan

1. Report of Kuropatkin to Nicholas II: "Vosstanie 1916 g.v Srednei Azii," op. cit., p. 80.

2. Report of the Dragoman of the Kashgar Consulate Stefanovich: *Vosstanie 1916 g.v Kirgizstane*, p. 110.

3. Broido, op. cit., p. 422.

(Syr Darya, Samarkand and Ferghana) were not affected inasmuch as not only were the number of Russians settled there small but moreover these were excused from military duty according to the provisions of the old law encouraging immigration into these areas by holding out this privilege to Russians born in these oblasts.

The effects of this corvée were especially felt in Semirechie which had a Russian population of 300,000. The Kazakhs and Kirghiz furnished workers for ploughing, harrowing, sowing, harvesting, and threshing on the fields of Russians away at the front. Where workers were not provided, each soldier's wife was given 18–25 roubles by the nomads for "assistance." There were cases where the "volunteer" workers received such shabby treatment that the authorities had to intercede. Thus in the village of Samsonovskoe they had to convince the soldiers' wives that they should feed their workers.[4]

In addition volunteer native groups were sent to the front as soldiers. The most notable case was that of the Tekke Turkomans. The Tekke Regiment covered itself with glory in the fighting at the front and was later to take part in Kornilov's unsuccessful *putsch* against the Kerensky government. The other volunteers came from among the Kirghiz. Whether these were actually volunteers is open to serious doubt. Kanaat Abukin, one of the leaders of the Kirghiz in the Revolt of 1916, asserts that they actually were assigned at the rate of several persons per volost and that in talking to them he learned that they did not go willingly but because the government demanded it.[5] This statement receives much support from the fact that the volunteers came precisely from those localities where the most serious excesses occurred in 1916.[6]

B. The Reaction of the Natives to the War

It would seem, at first glance, that the predominantly Moslem population of Russian Central Asia would prove a rich field for the

4. Ibid., p. 425.
5. Deposition of Kanaat Abukin: *Vosstanie 1916 g.v Kirgizstane*, p. 155.
6. Deposition of the engineer Tynyshpaev: ibid., p. 142.

intrigues and machinations of Turkish Pan-Islamic agents with the adherence of Turkey to the side of the Central Powers. The Turks certainly attempted to utilize the Pan-Islamic movement to stir up the Moslem peoples of the world against the Allied Powers. A legal opinion (*fetva*) was secured from the chief religious jurisconsult of the Ottoman Empire to the effect that military operations against the Allies would constitute a Jihad or holy war, though Turkey was fighting on the side of infidel Germany and Austria-Hungary. There were good grounds for this holy war in view of the fact that except for a few Moslems in Bosnia and East Africa all Moslems of the world not found under the rule of Moslems were included under the rule of the Allies.[7] Russia alone had two-thirds of the Turkish-speaking peoples of the world.

The material on the influence of Pan-Islamism in Russia during the war is not rich inasmuch as the movement developed in Turkistan almost without organization, without a systematic system of propaganda, and was expressed in an elemental form.

The difficulties facing the Turkistan Okhrana in combating Pan-Islamism are presented in a report of the Okhrana section head of Turkistan to the director of the department of police on May 21, 1915:

> The Moslem movement, affecting since the beginning of the war almost all the oblasts of the *krai* in one form or another but especially Ferghana, presents peculiarities owing to which the struggle with it must inevitably call for methods which are more complex than those in European Russia. The said movement has formed no organizations of the type we find in Russian revolutionary movements but those groups which we may call, by a stretch of the imagination, organizations with very few exceptions do not communicate by letter with each other or with alien groups, have no kind of written accounts of money they receive and expend and, thanks to the peculiarities of their national life, criminal meetings and gatherings plotting a great conspiracy are explained customarily in the event of disclosure as constituting . . . clubs and sometimes prayer meet-

7. A. J. Toynbee and K. P. Kirkwood, *Turkey* (London, 1926), p. 56.

ings while money gathered at meetings for the needs of Turkey in the event of disclosure is called private property. It is impossible to establish the existence of anything by witnesses as not one Moslem will testify against another.[8]

During the entire period from the beginning of the World War to the Revolt of 1916 the reports of the uezd heads, pristavs, and secret service agents are full of references to the appearance of Turkish agents and of meetings to gather money for Turkey. But seldom do we get concrete, specific instances. All this is usually reported "on rumour," "from conversations," from "transmissions," etc. The reports of the agents give a highly colored picture. Thus on January 10, 1915, one agent writes, "the Moslem population of the Andijan uezd are very sympathetic towards Turkey, dragged into war with Russia, and are trying to help her materially . . ." "The Ferghana oblast is seething with Afghan agents and there is not a village where they have not been . . ." "The native administration is completely solidified with the common mass."[9] Another agent writes, "Afghan emissaries are flooding Bukhara." "The Bukharians as a mass would like to eject the Russian *giaours* [unbelievers] from their government but know that they have not sufficient strength."[10]

The police, in an investigation in 1915, came upon hectograph copies of the following appeal:

> Moslems, the time has come to free ourselves of the Russian power. At the present time there rules over us the khalif of Islam, the Turkish sultan, carrying on war with Russia and the other powers. Every Moslem must aid this war and must make immediately an offering for its needs and for the good of all Islam. If anyone is not in the position to sacrifice then he must enter the ranks of the active army. The collected contribution is to be given to this representative and the appeal is to be circulated widely.[11]

8. A. Miklashevsky, "Sotsialnye dvizheniya 1916 g.v Turkestane," *Byloe*, no. 27–28 (1924), p. 243.
9. Events proved this quite untrue.
10. Miklashevsky, op. cit., p. 245.
11. Ibid., pp. 244–245.

Who was behind this appeal was never determined, though one of the great Andijan merchants became suspect and was exiled to Russia proper.

In February 1915 another appeal came into the hands of the Tsarist police. It read:

> The time has arrived to be freed from the rule of the unbeliever Russians. The Khalif has powerful allies. Help all that you can. These events were sent to the Moslems by God himself; therefore, he that will not help is an enemy of God. If force is not used now to free ourselves from the unbelievers then we will never be free.[12]

How accurate were the reports of the agents and officials, and did the appeals cited above testify to a dangerous and widespread movement in Turkistan? One of the communications of the Turkistan Governor-General in 1915 to the director of the Holy Synod tends to minimize the danger. "The native population react to the event—I have in mind the European war—indifferently and there can be danger only from the mullahs who may agitate in a manner undesirable for us."[13]

Careful consideration of the situation bears out that the Governor-General's report characterizes the temper of the people more accurately than those of the Okhrana agents. The latter seized upon the vaguest and wildest rumors of Pan-Islamic activity and reported them. Their reasoning was that by doing so they were showing their "zeal" and alertness. The Andijan affair had frightened the Tsarist government about the potentialities of Pan-Islamism in Turkistan. All foreigners were kept under strict surveillance and every effort was made to root out subversive activities. Despite the great efforts made, few concrete examples of plotting could be brought to light. If the plotting was as deep and widespread as the Okhrana agents reported, there certainly would have been more determined forms of expression. It took the supreme command for the conscription of native laborers in the rear to bring out an outburst of resistance. The eve of the announcement of mobilization found both the Sarts and nomads quiet and at peace.

12. Ibid., p. 244.
13. Ibid.

C. The Supreme Command of June 25

World War I caught the Russians with great gaps to be filled in their armament effort despite the fine work of the Duma beginning in 1908. The shortage was especially noticed in heavy artillery and shells. In the summer of 1915 the Russians could fire only a few hundred shells for every several thousand fired by the Germans. The output of rifles was far below actual needs and men were often sent to the front without arms. Whereas the lack of armament might be thought to limit the number of men under arms, in actuality it but increased reliance upon manpower. Fifteen million men were mobilized, withdrawing a third of the male productive force from factory and field. The entire period of Russian military operations on the Eastern front, from the frightful hecatombs of the Masurian Lakes and Tannenburg to the fall of the Tsarist government is a sickening tale of enormous lists of casualties—of the replacement of shells and guns as weapons by human beings. It is in this background of the ever-constant demand for human replacements and of a shortage of labor force as more males were called up that it was decided to call upon the native population of Russian Central Asia and the Caucasus to furnish men for work behind the front lines.

The entire question was decided at a meeting at the Stavka, the quarters of the commander-in-chief of the Armies.[14] General Alexeieff, the Chief of Staff, announced that he needed a levy of 500,000 men a month to cover the losses of the army. General Shuvaev, Minister of War, said he had only 1,175,000 persons in his reserve battalions, sufficing for only three months. The 600,000 men who could be secured from the five youngest age groups would require two months to train. All the generals present agreed that in view of the great urgency of the manpower question and the necessity to fill the places of those called from essential war work the labor levy of the Caucasian and Central Asian natives would have to take place on July 15.[15] The mobilization

14. The commander-in-chief at the time was Tsar Nicholas II himself.

15. Journal of Kuropatkin: "Vosstanie 1916 g.v Srednei Azii," op. cit., p. 48.

order was signed by Nicholas II on June 25: 250,000 natives were to be called from Central Asia from the 19–43 age bracket.

D. Meeting of the Governors of the Central Asian Krai

On the same day that the Tsarist supreme command was signed (June 25) there was called a special meeting of the military governors and other high officials of the Central Asian krai. This meeting was presided over by the acting Governor-General Erofeev and was called for the purpose of deciding by what means and manner the Tsarist order would be carried out.

The problem of how the natives were to be called was especially knotty, due to the fact that no record of births was kept among the population. Lieutenant General Galkin, the military governor of the Syr Darya oblast, expressed the opinion that, in view of the absence of birth certificates among the population, the requisition of workers strictly according to the instructions of the Ministry of the Interior was almost impossible as the administration did not have at its disposal the requisite forces while the very determination of the ages of the natives in the absence of birth certificates and in view of their practice of counting years by moon years and cycles would lead to malpractices on a mass scale. The call of workers by age group would lead them to think that they were being taken not as workers but as soldiers, thus causing agitation and even disorder. The call of the natives should be fulfilled by means familiar to the population and in such a manner as to obviate any misunderstanding. The call was to be represented as the fulfillment of a natural obligation on the part of the natives not different from tasks they already performed, such as corvée service for irrigation and road work and for the destruction of locusts. General Galkin thought that it was for the assembly only to determine the number of workers each oblast should give. The oblast governors, receiving from the assembly the number of workers they were to provide, were to apportion this number among the uezds, the uezds among the volosts, and so forth. In such a manner the task would be fulfilled easily and without complications. These views received the general assent of the assembly.

Another question discussed by the assembly was the probable attitude of the natives when informed about the conscription order. The consensus of those present was that there was no need to fear the outbreak of disorder. The governor of the Transcaspian oblast, Major General Kolmakov, asserted that there was no need to fear an uprising. He cited the examples of the Turkoman Tekke regiment performing such exemplary service at the front, and the many natives already sent to work on the Caucasus front. An appeal should be printed in the native newspapers explaining the aims of the mobilization order. Likoshin, the military governor of the Samarkand oblast, was of the opinion that no excesses need be expected if the call be presented as the fulfillment of natural duty by the natives.

General Gippius, the Governor of the Ferghana oblast, opined that the attitude of the masses depended upon that of the upper classes of the population, the mullahs, big merchants, landholders, etc. If the conscription order were carried out via the drawing up of family lists in which the ages of all the natives would be determined and all between the ages of 19 and 43 would be taken it would put the upper classes in a bad frame of mind as they would be taken also. Moreover the latter were physically weak and ill adapted for hard labor.

The Governor of the Syr Darya oblast concurred in the opinion that the conscription should be effected by order and not by family list.

Thus the authorities favored conscription by order and not by family lists for two reasons. In the first place it would require a great deal of time to prepare the lists of natives of the ages 19–43 and, in the second place, all upper-class natives who were in the subject age group would be included in the call. Under the plan favored by most of the assembly —the call of workers by order—the call to work would fall on definite individuals and not on a definite age group. Who these individuals would be was to be determined by the volost authorities. In this way the upper classes could be used in carrying out the conscription but would be themselves exempted.

Only one official spoke out against this scheme—a certain Bulatov by name. In his opinion the method was arbitrary and hence unjust and furthermore did not correspond to the supreme order which called for all natives 19–43 years old. With this opinion one other official concurred.

The assembly, however, recognized that conscription by order did not violate the supreme command, that the Ministries of War and the Interior by agreement left the method of determination of the ages to the assembly, that the method adopted would secure the workers with a minimum of time and effort. The selection of workers would be carried on with more equity if done by the natives themselves through their volost authorities than by Russian officials and, furthermore, if complaints of injustice arose they would be directed against their own officials and not at the Russians. Thus all the responsibility for future friction was laid on the shoulders of the native officials. They, on the other hand, received the widest scope for perpetrating injustices.[16]

The assembly then dealt with the problem of assigning to each oblast and each uezd the number of workers to be called.

According to the latest official figures the native non-Russian male population was about 3,500,000 (3,332,200). On the basis of this number the number of workers to be called from Turkistan (250,000) was about 8%,[17] of the total population, much higher in terms of males, 19–43 years old.

On the basis of this the figures to be assigned to the oblasts would be approximately:

Syr Darya	80,000
Ferghana	77,000
Semirechie	43,000
Samarkand	35,000
Transcaspia	15,000

The above distribution was obtained by apportioning the number of male natives each oblast contained as against the number of the

16. See Elaboration of the mobilization order: *Vosstanie 1916 g.v Kirgizstane*, pp. 17–22.

17. The khanates of Khiva and Bukhara are excluded. The order for mobilization did not apply to them.

entire krai. The assembly, however, did not confine itself to executing a mere mathematical exercise, but modified the break-down by oblast. What caused this modification was the desire to see that a sufficient labor force was left for the cotton-growing areas of Turkistan. Governor-General von Martsohn had telegraphed the assembly to that effect. Not only must a sufficient force be left for the gathering of the current cotton harvest but also for the cultivation of cotton in the coming year.

The conference pointed to the removal of prisoners of war from Turkistan to Siberia, once a source of labor as Turkistan had many German and Austrian prisoners of war. The number of workers from Persia, Afghanistan, and China was not great, and the number of native work hands did not suffice. The native women did not work in the fields while the Aulie-ata and Chernaevsky uezds had already provided 10,000 workers for work near the front. To secure a sufficient number of workers for the cotton industry the conference recognized that a reduction in the number of workers called for work behind the front lines from the cotton areas would have to be made at the expense of non-cotton areas. Ferghana oblast had the greatest area under cotton while Semirechie had none at all. Therefore Ferghana was to receive the greatest exemption of workers while Semirechie was to have the greatest additional conscription. With these considerations in mind the assembly redistributed the call for workers thus:

Syr Darya oblast		87,000
Semirechie	"	60,000
Ferghana	"	50,000
Samarkand	"	38,000
Transcaspia	"	15,000

Further, the assembly decided that areas in the uezds having 50% of their area under cotton would provide one-sixth of the workers that would be assigned to the area on the basis of the number of workers it had of the total male population of the krai. Areas having an acreage under cotton of 25–50% would provide one-third and areas under 25% would provide one-half.[18]

Finally the assembly recognized that a further reduction of workers for the cotton oblasts at the expense of the non-cotton oblasts would be inadmissible. In view of this and of the insufficiency of labor which threatened to develop even with the above changes the assembly asked the Governor-General to petition for a reduction of the workers demanded from Turkistan from 250,000 to 200,000.

Thus we see manifested a very great solicitude for the maintenance of the cotton acreage at its current figure. One Soviet writer asserts that the changes in the distribution were made after protests from officials of the cotton-growing districts in Turkistan, though the Moscow textile manufacturers were also much alarmed.[19]

The assembly also decided that the workers would be organized in echelons of from 1,400 to 1,500 persons. For each group of 200 persons there was to be appointed one individual, if possible from the workers themselves, to act as translator and elder. One mullah was authorized for each echelon to satisfy the religious needs of the workers.

E. The Revolt among the Sarts

The first phase of the Revolt of 1916 may be termed the revolt of the Sarts. Disorders and agitation began among both the Sarts and the nomads at approximately the same time, but the real trouble with the nomads was not to come until the beginning of August. By that time the Sarts had revolted and had been suppressed. The beginning of the revolt among the nomads found the Sarts broken and subdued; no further trouble was to come from them.

The order for mobilization struck a hard blow at the Sart peasant. He was to be mobilized at the very peak of the cotton harvest, when every hand was needed desperately. The economy was such that it called for little capital and much labor. A holding of 8 *tanaps* of land (2

18. Elaboration of mobilization order in *Vosstanie 1916 g.v Kirgizstane*, p. 23.

19. Introduction by Shestakov: "Dzhizakskoe vosstanie v 1916 g.," K.A. 5, no. 60 (1933), p. 61.

dessiatines) in Ferghana was not a small but an average holding and the taking away of a worker was nothing short of calamitous.[20] The situation for the peasant quite apart from any mobilization was desperate in 1916. The war had furthered the process of the replacement of land under food cultivation by land under cotton. In the war years the area under cotton rose from 567,000 dessiatines in 1914 to 714,000 dessiatines in 1916. The year 1915 was a record one for cotton, the harvest being 20.5 million puds. In 1916, because of a bad harvest the harvest was only 15 million puds, despite an extension of the cotton area.[21] Thus, though the peasant had increased his acreage of cotton, the bad harvest gave him no increase in production in 1916. What was worse, the decreased acreage under food, combined with the sluggish transport of grain from Siberia and Russia, brought high prices for food. Nor could the peasant find salvation in receiving a good price for his cotton crop. Cotton prices were fixed by the government during the war years at a low figure. According to the Ferghana governor this setting of prices "was decided with the presence of only one side, namely the representatives of factories and banks."[22] The upshot of the whole situation was that the peasant did not receive enough for his crop to pay his way and was forced to consume his meager working capital in order to stay alive. Needless to say the money lenders did very well in this situation.

The placing of the responsibility for the drawing up of lists of workers on the native officials provided them with a lever for extortion on a mass scale. Kerensky, sent by the Duma on a mission of investigation to Turkistan with another Duma member, revealed that he saw a 60-year-old man who "as a matter of fact appeared on the labor conscription list as 30 years old because he could not pay 300 roubles, while at the same time a young man, 25–30 years old, appeared as 50 because he was a rich person."[23] Speaking of these malpractices Gen-

20. Miklashevsky, op. cit., p. 248.

21. Shestakov, op. cit., pp. 88–89

22. Galuzo, op. cit., p. 155.

23. Ibid., pp. 153–154. *Alexander Kerensky* (1881–1970): Studied law at University of St. Petersburg where took degree. After graduation he joined the St. Petersburg bar where

eral Kuropatkin was to write in his journal, "It is difficult to establish how many bribes were taken in the single oblasts of Ferghana and Semirechie, especially by the officials of the native administration. The general sum must not be measured at other than millions of roubles. Complaints come from all sides."[24]

The order was announced to the population without any preparatory measures, causing incredible confusion. The wildest rumors were circulated. It was firmly believed by many that they were being taken as soldiers or that even if they were being taken as laborers, they would dig trenches under enemy fire in between the German and Russian forces.

An excellent account of the situation after the announcement of the conscription order is given by Lt. Col. Makkaveev, the Quartermaster General of the Turkistan krai. He writes in his "Short Survey of Events":

> The first days after the general notification to the natives (about the conscription order) passed with an outwardly peaceful deportment of the population but

---

he won a reputation as a defense counsel in political trials. In 1912 elected to the 4th Imperial Duma where he joined the Group of Toil (Labor) as his own party, the Social Revolutionaries, could not appear as an organized party. Won a reputation in the Duma by his fearless eloquence. After the overthrow of the Tsar became the vice president of the Petrograd Soviet and Minister of Justice in the Provisional Government, March 1917. Became Minister of War in May 1917 and set energetically to work to reorganize the army, reintroducing the death penalty. He was even able to launch a limited offensive in June under Allied pressure but this proved short lived due to the exhaustion of the army. Kerensky soon found himself caught between militarist reaction (the unsuccessful *putsch* of Kornilov) and the rising strength of the Bolsheviks culminating in the October Revolution and his government was characterized by vacillation and indecision. Other reasons standing in the background were: (1) the failure of his government to settle the agrarian problem, and (2) Kerensky's reluctance to shed blood by instituting a secret police to cope with the enemies of the government. (Perhaps St. Just was right when he remarked that "One cannot rule guiltlessly.") Kerensky escaped from Russia after the Bolshevik coup in October. He settled in Paris where he became the leader of the Social Revolutionary emigre group there, editing its paper, *Dni*, and writing books about the revolution. In 1940 Kerensky moved to Australia and in 1946 he came to the United States. Kerensky's brother, an engineer, was killed in Tashkent during the Bolshevik Revolution.

24. Journal of Kuropatkin: "Vosstanie 1916 g.v Srednei Azii," op. cit., p. 51.

> there was noticed everywhere among them a deep agitation: they deserted the bazaars, gatherings for nightly celebrations during the Moslem fast in force at the time almost ceased, the mass of the population gathered only in the mosques for prayer . . . ; there appeared signs of a general link among the main centres of Mohammedanism in the country and there appeared even rumors of a future general uprising of Moslems, supposedly on the 18th of July, the first day of the holiday Aidi-Fitr. Although the official and influential persons among the natives recognized the necessity for the workers to obey the order, nevertheless they did not hide the fact that the population was agitated and was hostilely disposed towards the demands of the order; several petitions were presented for the substitution of the natural duty by a pecuniary one . . . After cases of disorders the well-to-do natives of Tashkent and Samarkand began to remove their families from the city and to hide their most valuable goods in gardens and in the suburbs. According to the information of the political agent in Bukhara messengers rode out from Samarkand on July 7 to Afghanistan with a request for aid . . .[25]

In Tashkent agents of the Okhrana reported rumors that the poor would settle accounts with the rich if the latter were given the right to buy their way out of the conscription. The rumor that a general uprising was to break out on July 18 caused a near panic among the Russians scattered over the country. Both they and the administration besought the government for arms to use against the imminent attack. In the places the nomads occupied there took place a migration of auls away from the cities. These peoples started moving into the steppes, the hills, and the border areas (especially to Chimkent uezd, Turkistan,[26] Perovsk, Kazalinsk, the Hungary Steppes, the border regions of Transcaspia, Semirechie) and even out of the Russian Empire.[27]

The first outburst among the Sarts took place on July 4 in the city of Khojent. Here a huge crowd fell upon a guard post in order to secure

25. Quoted in Shestakov, op. cit., p. 91.

26. The city of Turkistan (also called Azret), not to be confused with the region of Turkistan.

27. Miklashevsky, op. cit., p. 249.

arms. The crowd was dispersed by shooting into it. The date of the attack is significant. Since the order for conscription was not announced to the population until July 8, it shows that the population already knew of the order before its announcement.

On July 7 in the village of Dagbit, Samarkand uezd, a native crowd fell upon the volost head, the scribe, and jigits (mounted native messengers and scouts) and killed them. The list of workers to be called, made up for the volost, was destroyed. Simultaneously on July 9 there occurred disorders in the city of Andijan. In Andijan the students of the medresseh started a demonstration against conscription. Troops were sent to break up the crowd. Shots were fired and ten natives were badly wounded. This only served to infuriate the crowd which began to struggle with the police and Cossacks, throwing sticks and rocks at them. This attack was dispersed by gunfire, leaving 12 natives wounded. One Cossack and several policemen were also wounded in the scuffle.

The movement in Ferghana spread from the cities to the rest of the oblast. There occurred in a series of settlements the killing of volost heads, scribes, and jigits. The individual movements were directed primarily at the police and native officialdom and had as their goal the stoppage of the drawing up of lists of workers to be called.[28]

On July 11 disorders took place in the cities of Namangan and Dalverzan, Ferghana oblast. The official report of the assistant uezd head describes the events that took place in the city of Namangan:

> Around 8:00 a.m. the police chief of the third district let me know by telegraph that disorders had begun among the natives in his district. Arriving there immediately with a detachment of police I saw in the area around the water hole a crowd of several thousand persons, among whom women were present. The crowd literally roared not hearing any admonitions which caused me to call for a detachment of troops with machine guns. With the appearance of the troops the crowd calmed down a bit giving opportunity to deliver admonitions. I, myself,

28. Report of Kuropatkin to Nicholas II: "Vosstanie 1916 g.v Srednei Azii," op. cit., p. 68.

knowing the native tongue asked the crowd not to create mischief, to conduct itself peacefully so as not to call forth severe measures. From the crowd there were heard voices: "If the troops are taken away the crowd will disperse." The troops were removed but the crowd began to agitate even more, pressed towards the police and demanded the destruction of the lists that had been drawn up; the troops appeared again. Inasmuch as talk had no effect on the crowd it was necessary to threaten that armed force would be employed but with that threat the crowd did not calm down but, on the contrary, began to behave in an even more defiant manner. Hearing threatening cries of "*ur*"[29] the crowd moved forward towards the assembled platoon standing at trail arms and began to go for the firearms, the sabers of the police, and the two machine guns set in front of the platoon. Though thrice being warned that they would be fired upon the crowd pressed forward. Volleys were fired and only after this were the mutineers dispersed.[30]

In the village of Dalverzan the volost head had announced the mobilization order to the people. They greeted this announcement with defiant cries and when the volost head started to place his seal on the order to the effect it had been announced, the crowd pressed towards him. The volost head tried to defend himself by shooting, but the infuriated mob killed him and two jigits. There were no troops to call in the immediate area so that the crowd broke up of its own accord and went home.

By July 13 the movement had seized all of Ferghana oblast. On July 17 the entire Turkistan krai was placed under martial law. All civil departments were placed in subordination to the commander of the armies. The latter immediately issued orders calling for (1) the formation of provisional military courts, (2) that the administration should report three times a day regarding the disposition of the population, (3) the dispersal of all "native mobs" in the zone of the railway by armed force.

The actions of General Gippius, the Governor of the Ferghana oblast, were, to say the least, most erratic. He announced that Tashkent had wrongly interpreted the supreme command, that in reality the command applied only to those who *wanted* to go to work in the

29. *Ur* = kill.
30. See Miklashevsky, op. cit., p. 260.

rear of the front lines. He announced this to the natives in thousands of appeals which he distributed over Ferghana oblast. He told Erofeev, the commander of the army in Turkistan, that his orders were leading to rebellion and announced that he was going to deal directly with the Premier, the Minister of War, and others. Gippius was of the opinion that if the good will of the natives were cultivated, if their patriotism were appealed to, they would volunteer in greater numbers than were needed.[31] On July 13 he appeared before a crowd of natives in Namangan dressed in native khalat or gown and skull cap holding a copy of the Koran in his hands. He read appropriate passages and kissed the holy book. "In this holy book," he declared, "there is told of the necessity to help the White Tsar against the Germans." According to Okhrana archives this produced a strong impression on the natives.

This attempt to get the natives to volunteer, however, proved a complete failure. Gippius issued further appeals but to no avail. Finally on July 16 he announced that the call would be postponed until September 15 in order to give the natives a chance to harvest their crops. According to one Soviet writer[32] he was prompted to do this by the Moscow committee of the Bourse who impressed upon him the necessity to save the cotton crop. He sent the latter the following telegram: "Despite the declaration of martial law in the Turkistan military *okrug* [district] I beg you to calm the commercial class regarding conditions in the Ferghana oblast. The outburst of disorders, occasioned by a perverted interpretation of the supreme command regarding the call of workers, is quickly being subdued under the influence of my oral and written explanations, life is getting back to normal and I will soon present a petition for the removal of martial law in Ferghana oblast."[33]

In reality the disorders not only continued but grew worse, making removal of martial law unthinkable. The effects of martial law had a very unfavorable effect upon cotton production in Ferghana oblast. The imposition of martial law interfered with the transport of cotton as all

31. Kuropatkin's Journal: "Vosstanie 1916 g.v Srednei Azii," op. cit., p. 47.

32. Shestakov, op. cit., p. 92.

33. Ibid., p. 92.

transport of freight and people was regulated. The peasants were placed in a very unfavorable position inasmuch as the banks and commercial houses ceased to give them the usual advances on their crop. As an upshot of the whole débâcle Gippius was forced to turn in his resignation.

In the Syr Darya oblast an additional irritant was provided by the high price of grain owing to the drought which was felt here more acutely than in the other oblasts of Turkistan. Opposition was expressed in a very elemental form and was confined to resistance to the drawing up of lists of workers subject to the call, during which six native officials were killed. Even the disorders which took place in Old Tashkent[34] on July 11 were significant only for the effect they had on the natives elsewhere, especially in Jisak.

On July 11 the *piatidesyatniki* or heads of 50 households of Tashkent were called together by the authorities for the purpose of explaining to them what the call was all about and how the lists were to be drawn up. An ever-increasing crowd began to form around the police building where this was taking place. In the crowd were many Moslem women, a feature characteristic of these demonstrations. The crowd began to demand that a halt be put to the drawing up of lists of workers. Their threats not having any effect, the mood of the crowd became ugly. They attempted to enter the building but the police barred the way. The crowd then killed the native guard outside, and someone seized a revolver from a policeman. The police fired into the crowd and then barricaded themselves inside the building. The crowd knocked

34. As in Europe the introduction of the railways into Turkistan was regarded by many of the local inhabitants with superstitious fear and suspicion. In consideration of the susceptibilities of the latter railway stations were erected and the railway routed a discreet distance from cities by the Russians. The commercial revolution brought by the railway convinced many of the local merchants that their future was bound up with that of the railway with the result that many commercial companies transferred their headquarters from the old city to the new one being built around the railway station. In this way there resulted "new" and "old" cities along the Transcaspian railway, the first dynamic, growing, and made up of a mixed Russian and local population—similar to the mushroom towns in the early days of the American West—the second, old, tradition-bound, and often declining as progressive elements transferred their activities to the new city.

out the windows and tore down the communication wires leading to the building. Troops finally arrived and the crowd was dispersed. Four people were killed and six wounded.

The Tashkent affair was of very small dimensions compared to the greatness of the city. Its chief significance lay in the fact that the disorders took place in the capital of the krai, the very nerve centre of the administration. Exaggerated rumors of what took place greatly encouraged natives elsewhere as they thought the capital was with them.

The course of the disorders in the three basic oblasts was stereotyped and did not provide a wide variety of form. The movements showed little organization or range. The usual sequence of events was that a crowd would assemble before the village or volost chancellery and ask to see the authorities about the meaning of the order. When the authorities appeared, they would demand that the drawing up of lists be stopped. When this was refused, bloody events would occur. Troops would then arrive and disperse the crowd by force of arms.[35]

Events in the Samarkand oblast took the traditional form of resistance described above, except in the uezd of Jizak. Here the movement was expressed in a much more advanced form both as to extent and intensiveness. General Kuropatkin was to term this "open revolt" and so it was indeed.[36]

The Jizak uezd was primarily a grain-producing area. Also of importance were gardening and especially viniculture. It had greater opportunities of cultural and political development than many of the other Sart areas. It was situated near the great centres of the krai (Tashkent, Khojent, and Samarkand), had the railway running through its territory and was near the irrigated fringe of the Hungary Steppe. There was undoubtedly a tie between the Bukharan Pan-Islamists and the cultured circles of Jizak though precise information on this score is lacking.[37]

The absence of such an intensive culture of cotton in Samarkand

35. Miklashevsky, op. cit., p. 259.

36. Report of Kuropatkin to Nicholas, "Vosstanie 1916 g.v Srednei Azii," op. cit., p. 61.

37. "Dzhizakskoe vosstanie 1916 g.," op. cit., p. 61

oblast as there was in Ferghana was to have an unfavorable effect upon the number of conscript workers it was to furnish. As has already been noted, the special assembly of the Turkistan upper officialdom, because of this fact, was to raise the number of workers to be furnished by Samarkand oblast from an original 35,000 to 38,000, while the cotton-raising districts in each oblast were to furnish fewer workers than the grain-producing districts. Jizak, being a grain-producing area, thus suffered doubly; it was ordered to furnish 10,600 persons.

A less immediate though equally important cause for dissatisfaction among the population was the seizure of land in connection with the irrigation of the Hungary Steppe. This operation was the pet project of the Grand Duke Nicholas K. Romanov, a cousin of the Tsar, banished to Turkistan because of past indiscretions. Land was seized, water rights usurped, and the population was barred even from securing firewood in the woods, the latter a serious matter as winters in Turkistan are quite cold. In addition to the Sart agricultural economy the Jizak area included a well-developed Kazakh cattle-raising economy. The Kazakhs were squeezed out from the best pasture lands into the barren hills.

The movement in Jizak uezd began on July 2, 1916. On that date the Russian authorities gathered representatives of the population in old Jizak and announced the mobilization order to them. Thirteen Sarts were singled out, the responsibility of furnishing the required workers was placed on them, and they were given ten days to present the workers. The work of drawing up the lists was performed by the piatidesyatniki or *Illik-bashi* together with the Russian authorities. The lists were drawn up in such a way that the sons of "bais" and of the authorities were left off while the great percentage of those on the lists was made up of the sons of the poor. On July 12 the pristav and doctors arrived to begin the processing of workers in Old Tashkent. The call was completed for one section of the city and was to begin in another the next day. On July 12 there appeared among the assembled workers a certain Nazir Khoja Abdusalyamov, an ishan who had been to Tashkent to find out the situation there and who had just returned. He reported that Tashkent had decided to revolt rather than furnish workers. With this information in hand the workers called a meeting for the evening of July 12 where it was decided to take away the lists of workers to be called. This was accomplished on the morning of the 13th. During the proceedings Mirza Yar Khudoyarov, the district bailiff, was murdered after threatening the crowd with his revolver.

The *gazavat* or holy war was then announced and Nazir Khoja was proclaimed *bek*. The crowd, armed with sticks, knives, sickles, etc. headed towards new Jizak to demand that the conscription be stopped. Nazir Khoja walked at the head of the mob. Colonel Rukin, the uezd head, rode out from new Jizak to meet the mob. He attempted to pacify the crowd by saying that the mobilization would be stopped but the crowd did not believe him. He was pulled down from his horse and killed as was Captain Zotoglov, the pristav of the region, and a jigit who accompanied him. The crowd then continued on their way to Jizak but meeting the fire of the troops there they retreated to the old city. Here they prepared themselves for the coming battle. They gathered together what arms they had, stored provisions, and mobilized all artisans for the making of swords, axes, and other crude weapons.

The Russians, few in number, shut themselves up in the new city's barracks. The insurgents, not meeting any resistance, went for the railway installations where, under the direction of the native railway workers employed on repairing operations, they indulged in an orgy of destruction. They destroyed the railway lines, bridges, and telegraph lines in the direction of station Somakin. All the railway line from Jizak to Obruchev, a distance of 65 versts, was torn up. Sixteen Russian railway workers were killed and an attack was made on the trains.

The Russian population remained all night in the encampment guarding themselves with outposts and patrols. The next day saw the arrival of a detachment under a Colonel Afanasev which managed to confine the rebellion to the old city.

The news of the uprising in the city of Jizak caused rebellion to start in other points of the uezd. The main participants were the Uzbeks of the Sansar river valley and around Zaamin and Bogdan. Somewhere rifles appeared and beks[38] were proclaimed. Bands were formed, significant in number but poorly armed. The object of the rebellion was not only the stopping of the conscription but, if successful, complete independence from Russia. There was hope of aid from Afghanistan and Germany. In the Sanzar district a native judge, Turadbekov, was proclaimed Khan.

In the Bogdan district one Abdurakhman Abujabarov Jevachi was proclaimed Khan and declared holy war against the Russians. He agreed to act together with Nasir Khoja against the Russians. An expedition was organized to come to the aid of Jizak.

As soon as Tashkent heard of the events in Jizak a special punitive force was dispatched from Tashkent and Samarkand. It was made up of 13 companies, 6 cannon, 3 *sotnias* of Cossacks, and three-fourths of a company of sappers. To this infantry force there was added a large cavalry detachment, the horses and saddles for which were obtained by requisition.

Part of this force was assigned to guard the railway, a small garrison was left in Jizak, while the rest of the force was divided into five flying columns whose mission it was to scatter and punish the insurgents. The latter were powerless against such a force though some further resistance was put up and an attempt made to tear up railway lines. The Russians retook the Russian settlement of Zaamin near the railway lines which had been taken by the insurgents. July 16 saw the restoration of the railway and telegraph lines in all the uezd and from that date there was communication between Tashkent and Jizak. The followers of the various native leaders gradually began to return to the village. Some fled to the hills but were pursued and forced into submission by three Cossack columns sent against them. Others tried to break through to Bukhara and Afghanistan. Abdurakhman Abujabarov

38. *Bek* (beg) A Turkish title, Ottoman *bey*, Kirghiz bī or *biy*. The various meanings given to this word may be summarized in three categories: (1) A *beg* is a noble in distinction to the common people; also the ruling princes. (2) The "prince" of a small tribe or area in contradistinction to the *khan*, the ruler of a larger area. (3) Any "position of authority" may carry this title, from the head of a village to a governor of an area. The earliest Turkic inscriptions use the word *beg* in all three meanings. See article on "bek," *Encyclopaedia of Islam*, vol. I, p. 689.

surrendered, Nazir Khoja was captured in the steppe after being given up by Kazakhs not taking part in the revolt, while Turadbekov succeeded in hiding himself. By the 26th or the 27th of July the uprising was crushed and the natives agreed to furnish the workers demands.

The goal of the punitive unit under Colonel Ivanov was not only to pacify the natives but to impress upon them a lesson that they would not soon forget. One of the survivors of the pacification relates:

> Ivanov[39] gave the order to shoot, burn, confiscate household goods and agricultural implements. The units went to the *kishlaks*,[40] burned goods, whomever they met they shot, women were raped and other bestialities perpetrated. In the kishlaks they burned the growing crops while the ready grain was taken away. The population fled to the city, to the steppe, leaving behind their property. Hunger began. The women fled leaving behind the children. The refugees starved in the far-away steppes and in the cities.[41]

In addition the field courts set up dealt summarily with the many arrested persons brought in.

Finally on August 20 General Kuropatkin arrived in Jizak. After visiting the graves of the fallen Russian officials he assembled the influential natives and told them: "It would be best to hang all of you but we are allowing you to live so that you may be a warning example to others. The place where Col. Rukin was killed is to be enclosed for a radius of 5 versts. This will belong to the government. The people inhabiting this territory are to be ejected immediately."[42] Shades of Andijan!

In addition to the Russians mentioned above, the insurgents killed the Zaamin pristav, Sobolev, the inhabitants of the Russian settlement of Zaamin, members of the Forest Service, and a party of statisticians of the Ministry of Agriculture. The total Russian loss was 83 killed, 20 wounded. Seventy Russians were taken into captivity, mostly women and children, the majority of the women being raped. The property

39. Later Minister of War under Kolchak in Siberia in 1918.
40. *Kishlak* = Sart village.
41. Introduction, "Dzhizakskoe vosstanie 1916 g.," op. cit., p. 63.
42. Ibid., p. 63.

damage to the Russians was estimated at 1 million roubles though Kuropatkin thought this figure was probably exaggerated.[43]

One of the most significant actions of the Jizak insurgents, pointing to the great power of the movement, was the destruction of the railway; neither in Ferghana nor Samarkand was the railway destroyed. In view of the wretchedness of the Turkistan roads[44] this was a matter of crucial importance for the success of any rebellion. The Russians were completely dependent upon the railway for rapid transfer of troops from one point to another. If the railway had been cut in localities other than around Jizak the rebellion would have been much more difficult to suppress.

From all information, the fact that the Jizak movement reached such proportions as it did was due to the fact that the initial act of resistance to the Russians—the murder of Colonel Rukin, the uezd head—was not countered by immediate punitive measures. Success inspired and strengthened the belief of the people in themselves. They set out to accomplish two goals: (1) destroy the railway and thus prevent the dispatch of Russian troops against them, and (2) exterminate the Russian oppressors. Locally these efforts met with success; only with the arrival of troops from the outside, armed with cannon and machine guns, did the movement collapse.

Despite the greater depth and intensity of the Jizak revolt it was characterized by the fitting of means to the end only during the revolt itself; there was no master plan carefully conceived long before the revolt. "When the mass threatened the uezd Nachalnik hardly a single

43. "Report of Kuropatkin to Nicholas II, "Vosstanie 1916 g.v Srednei Azii," op. cit., p. 67.

44. Skobelev, the conqueror of the Turkomans, wrote in 1877: "if known to Dante the Central Asian road would have served as an additional horror to hell." Curzon, op. cit., p. 400. Colonel Bailey, speaking of his experiences as a British agent in Turkistan during the Bolshevik revolution, writes: "Russian Turkistan is in one way a curious country. Railways were made before roads—at least before respectable roads. The result is that when the railway line was cut by the enemy [the White forces under General Dutov] there was not, as one might have expected, any possibility of communication by car. In fact, motor cars could only travel short distances from Tashkent." F. M. Bailey, op. cit., p. 36.

individual consciously acted towards any kind of goal; the mass was under the influence of the moment, the individual under the influence of the mass."[45] They were inflamed by Nazir Khoja, himself too much under the fresh impression of the Tashkent disorders to appraise the situation correctly.

The Jizak revolt had a direct resemblance to the Andijan uprising. In both affairs beks were proclaimed, a holy war announced, and the white banner of national liberation raised. Both were non-radical movements led by remnants of the old feudal religious classes. While Nazir Khoja[46] was an ishan with modest property the other leaders like Kasin Khoja in Zaamin and Muktav in Jizak were wealthy landowners. Turadbekov was of bek origin. The bulk of the movement was made up of the peasantry. While economic reasons were behind much of the peasants' dissatisfaction, their leaders, as in the Andijan uprising, used this resentment to stir them up against the Russians without planning to initiate economic reforms for their benefit in case of success. These leaders were wholly ignorant of the great changes that had been effected by capitalism and failed to realize that they could not turn back the clock to khanate days.

Religious fanaticism was undoubtedly one of the chief agents motivating the revolt. The outbreak of disorders in the city of Jizak found many medresseh (Moslem religious academy) students in the crowd which clashed with the Tsarist forces. The declaration of the holy war has already been noted.

The Jizak uprising differed from that of Andijan in one respect—it saw the introduction of a new force—the native railway workers. The great difference in pay, working conditions, and employment between native and Russian workers, especially on the railway, has already been noted. This undoubtedly served as an incentive in causing them to join the insurgent forces.

45. Miklashevsky, op. cit., p. 262.

46. Nazir Khoja was an agent of a Jizak dealer in millstones. He owned a small house and 4 tanaps of land in Jizak, valued at 2,000 roubles.

F. The Appointment of General Kuropatkin as Governor-General

The final suppression of the disorders among the Sart population roughly coincides with the appointment of General Kuropatkin, who received his appointment on July 21. The disorders were suppressed and the conscription of workers among the Sarts started in the closing days of July.

The actions of General Erofeev, the acting Governor-General, had since the beginning of the disorders been directed towards pacifying the population by brute force rather than by explaining the order to the natives or eradicating any of the abuses. He tried to show in his telegrams to Petrograd that his measures were having their desired effect but after each such telegram he had to report new disorders and murders of Russians.

Kuropatkin believed that the basis for his new appointment was served by his forwarding of a telegram from the khansha Guldzhemal of the Tekke Turkomans to Alexeieff, Chief of Staff of the Army, and copies to the Ministers of the Interior and of War. The telegram asked Kuropatkin to intercede in the call of the Turkomans as laborers. The Turkoman population had, without the slightest warning, been called to furnish workers by July 15, precisely the time the cotton crop was to be harvested. The concluding words of the telegram were these:

> Any possible delay in the conscription of the Tekkes may be interpreted in a sense unfavorable for the Tekkes and in that case they are threatened with severe military repression. From the time of the arrival of your nachalniks in the Transcaspian oblast the Tekke people and I personally have been accustomed to turn to you as to a father for all national needs, be they large or small. Now in the sight of unparalleled misfortune threatening the Tekke tribes I turn to your Excellency as the representative of the Tekkes of the Merv uezd with the fervent prayer to intercede before His Imperial Highness concerning the suspension of the calling of workers until the end of the cotton harvest or until a time that would give all Tekkes the opportunity to accustom themselves to the concept of their new duty and to work out the fulfillment of it among individuals in consonance with the demands of justice.[47]

47. Journal of Kuropatkin: "Vosstanie 1916 g.v Srednei Azii," op. cit., p. 46.

The telegram was forwarded to the above-mentioned officials together with a request by Kuropatkin for the Emperor to postpone the calling of the Tekkes till September 15.

On the morning of July 21 the Minister of War, Shuvaev, contacted the Emperor and told him that in view of the serious disorders that had broken out in Turkistan he was asking that Kuropatkin be appointed to the Governor-Generalship in Turkistan to pacify the population. This proposition the monarch did not accept. A second report by Shuvaev, however, caused the Tsar to write out at 4:00 p.m. a supreme command for the desired appointment. When Kuropatkin heard of the appointment he asked that he be given the powers of commander-in-chief in Turkistan to which the Emperor agreed.

Kuropatkin remained in Petrograd for a few weeks, not arriving in Tashkent until August 8. Before leaving Petrograd he received a visit from a General Pokotillo, who had just returned from Turkistan and who knew the region well. The latter painted a not too flattering picture of the officials in command there. He reported in part that "Martsohn, the Governor-General, has gone to pieces. The Syr Darya Governor-General, Galkin, is drunk every day. The Samarkand one, Likotin, is blind. The Ferghana one—Gippius—is crazy. The Transcaspian—Kolmakov—weak, without a will, the Semirechie—Folbaum—better than the others. The head of the chancellery, Efremov, who meddles in everything, is very suspect and, it appears, manages affairs fraudulently. The assistant Governor-General, Erofeev, is very inexperienced," and so on.[48]

The bulk of Kuropatkin's actions belong to the second phase of the revolt and will be considered there. It is to this phase that we now turn.

48. Ibid., p. 46.

5

The Revolt of 1916: Second Phase

A. The Revolt of the Kirghiz and Kazakhs

1. The Announcement of the Supreme Order

The circumstances surrounding the announcement of the mobilization of workers to the Kirghiz and Kazakh peoples and the reaction that followed was much the same as among the Sart population although resistance took much longer to crystallize definitely. As with the Sarts, there was no preparatory work undertaken to soften the blow or to present in a patriotic light the sacrifice the natives would make for the war effort. This absence of preparatory steps was recognized by the highest officials of the country. Thus in July 1916 the Viceroy of the Caucasus, the Grand Duke Nicholai Nicholaievich, sought a change in conscription orders as applied to the country entrusted to him on the ground that "any measures affecting the Moslem population require for their fulfillment a series of preparatory measures which in their turn require considerable time."[1] On July 31 Kuropatkin wrote in his journal: "Stürmer [Prime Minister] and Shuvaev [the War Minister] did all that was possible to stir up the population. The order for the call of the natives to work was given by Stürmer without interrogation of the officials on the spot and without receiving from them

1. Foreword by A. Chuloshnikov, "K istorii vosstaniya kirghiz v 1916 g," op. cit., p. 53.

their opinion concerning the arrangements and dates for the fulfillment of the call for natives to work."[2]

One of the *bon mots* which made the rounds of St. Petersburg society before the first World War was that "Russia has departments but no government." The first attempts at fulfilling the order for conscription of workers were to prove that there was much truth in this quip. The successful fulfillment of the order was predicated upon the coordination of the activities of the Ministry of War and the Ministry of the Interior. Such coordination there was not. On the day following the announcement of the supreme command the Minister of the Interior telegraphed to the governors of the oblasts affected that they should begin the mobilization of the first contingent of Kazakhs and Kirghiz, 18–25 years old, in the shortest space of time.

On the spot there was complete confusion, the degree of which may be gathered from the case of Sokolovsky, the Astrakhan Governor. In conformity with the instructions of the Minister of the Interior Sokolovsky brought all the forces and means he had at his disposal towards the calling up of his first contingent of natives on July 10. This call he was forced to cancel after receiving a telegram from the Ministry of the Interior which declared that the War Department was seriously hampering the transport of the native workers.

Sokolovsky then entered into relations with the staff of the Kazan military *okrug* or district. On July 23 he received from the Astrakhan uezd military head the statement that he could accept daily 1,000 natives beginning with August 5. Sokolovsky thereupon issued a second call for workers but on July 26 he was told by the uezd head to postpone the reception of workers until a plan of transportation was received from the War Department. "Thus in a short time I was twice forced to announce a call and twice to rescind the order," Sokolovsky stated.[3] Sokolovsky considered this situation very harmful for all concerned.

2. Journal of Kuropatkin: "Vosstanie 1916 g.v Srednei Azii," op. cit., pp. 45–46.

3. Telegram of Sokolovsky to director of Zemsky div., "K istorii vosstaniya kirghiz v 1916 g.," op. cit., p, 36.

The natives had to traverse as many as 300 *versts* to get to the collecting stations and then to go home to await another call, thus causing needless economic loss. Furthermore this might be interpreted as showing the weakness and vacillation of the Russian government and thus give agitators a chance to stir up the native peoples.

As with the Sarts, the conscription order became a lever for mass extortion and malpractice on the part of the native administration. Bribes were taken to keep natives off the list. Volost heads used the order to settle accounts with their party enemies, including all of their antagonists in the age group 19–31, the first contingent. Or they might be denounced as opposing the government and brought before the Russian authorities. The rich Kirghiz in preparing the lists wrote the ages of their sons older than they actually were so that there were cases of 20-year-old *bits* or native judges (officials exempt from the conscription order) when the law required they be no younger than 25.[4] When faced with injustice the population often took the law into its own hands which usually took the form of taking the lists away from the volost head. This occurred in the Turgai, Uralsk, Akmolinsk, Semipalatinsk, and Semirechie oblasts. Other native authorities, fearing violence from the Kirghiz youth, fled to Russian centres like Uralsk and Ilek and there made up their lists in extraordinary circumstances.

The same wild rumors were circulated as to the real object of the conscription as among the Sarts. The illiterate translators, forced to translate expressions they had never heard before, such as "requisition," "defense construction in the theater of military operations," "military communications," did so incorrectly and bluntly, leaving the impression that the Kirghiz and Kazakhs were being taken as soldiers directly to the front without any military training. Or if it was believed that they were taken as workers there were repeated the assertions that they would dig trenches in between the Germans and Russians while the latter fired at each other. In Semirechie the Russian

4. Protocol of the informal meeting of Kirghiz [Kazakhs], ibid., p. 58.

peasants told the Kirghiz that they were being sent to the front to die and that the peasants would then seize their land. The very term "requisition," *rekvizitsia*, used in the official documents in connection with the conscription of workers, offended the natives' sensibilities.[5]

If the conscription call caught the Sarts in the middle of the cotton harvest, the call among the Kirghiz and Kazakhs caught many of them, especially the Kazakhs, in the middle of agricultural operations. In the northern uezds of the Steppe oblasts the Kazakhs lived interspersed among the Russians on farms not dissimilar to those of the Russian peasants and needing workers just as much as the peasant farms. In the Uralsk, Aktiubinsk, Kustanaisk, Petropavlovsk, Kokchetavsk, Omsk, Akmolinsk, Pavlodarsk, Semipalatinsk, Barnaul, Ust Kamenogorsk, and Zaisan uezds the Kirghiz and Kazakhs were the only labor force left, because of the absence of the Russian peasants at the front. The call caught them in the midst of haying and on the eve of the harvest of grain.

In some localities it was believed that the call was voluntary, inasmuch as the people had been told that they paid the various numerous taxes and contributions since the beginning of the war in lieu of military service. Others believed that the order conscription was entirely the work of the local authorities to show their zeal to the central government and thereby receive promotions by forcing the Kirghiz to become volunteers. The Kirghiz based this conviction on the knowledge that the Przhevalsk uezd head had demanded in the previous year that some Kirghiz volunteer for service in the active army.[6]

The movement of protest against the malpractices of their volost officials by the Kirghiz and Kazakhs brought the first appearance of Cossack detachments in a generation. The burden of feeding these forces was placed upon the local native communities. The official report of the informal meeting of the steppe peoples on August 7, 1916, thus characterizes the results of this intrusion:

5. G. Stepnyak, "Kirgizskoe vosstanie v Semipalatinskoi gubernii v 1916 godu," *Sibirskie ogni*, vol. I (1928), p. 133.

6. Deposition of Kanaat Abukin: *Vosstanie 1916 g.v Kirgizstane*, p. 155.

> The appearance in the steppe of the Cossack units brought terror to the peaceful population of the great region. The Kirghiz [Kazakhs] up till this time peacefully awaiting the call of the subject workers, became agitated: in places leaving all of their property, selling the land for a song, they went away to the south. The youths left the auls, went into the steppe, and it is unknown where they are. Everywhere the Kirghiz left the ripening grain; the cut hay remains in heaps, rots, and is carried away by the wind. The economy is dealt an irreparable blow seeing that from the time of the announcement of the call no one has been occupying himself with agricultural matters. In the Urzhavsk volost of the Lepsinsk uezd of the Semirechie oblast the Kirghiz, going no one knows where, poisoned their grain and hay for the cattle.[7]

Whereas conscription in any form had been totally unexpected for the Sarts, among the nomads, especially the Kazakhs, the question had been in the air for some time. M. Tynyshpaev,[8] an influential Kazakh among the native intelligentsia, tells how Chaev, the director of military construction works, approached him in September 1915 to learn his opinion concerning a project to call up the Kazakhs as soldiers. Tynyshpaev expressed his opinion and wrote about the project to the editor of the *Kazak*.

> In December 1915 this project was discussed in the press. On Jan. 24, 1916, the paper *Kazak* (no. 166) gave the opinions of some influential Kirghiz [Kazakhs] as to the question of the expected placing of military service on the Kirghiz; the question of the desire or lack of desire to serve in the army was not considered at all; all interested themselves in the question of how the Kirghiz would serve—in the infantry or the cavalry, the question being thrashed out on the pages of the *Kazak* nos. 166, 168, 177, 179, 184--the last of June 9 . . . In general the articles of the said numbers may be summarized thus: (1) the majority of the Kirghiz prefer

7. Protocol of the informal meeting of the Kirghiz and Kazakhs at Turgai: "K istorii vosstaniya kirghiz v 1916 g.," op. cit., p. 59.

8. Tynyshpaev, belonging to the Kazakh bai-manap class, was leader of the Semirechie Alash Orda. He was educated as an engineer, attending school at St. Petersburg. As deputy from the Semirechie oblast in the 2nd Imperial Duma he adhered to the Cadet faction. During the Revolt of 1916 he accompanied General Kuropatkin in his tour of the country as interpreter. He became a commissar under the Provisional Government and later member of the "government of Kokand autonomy" in Turkistan, 1917–1918.

> service in the cavalry (including myself), the minority stood for service in the infantry. (2) It is proposed that in view of the absence of birth certificates among the Kirghiz the call for military service in the near future will be beset with many difficulties.[9]

On February 3, 1916, to enquire into the whole question of the conscription of the Kirghiz and Kazakh a group made up of A. Bukeikhanov,[10] leader of the Alash Orda, A. Baitursunov, editor of the *Kazak*, and N. Begymbetov set out for Petrograd. While in Petrograd they visited several persons including General Polivanov, then Minister of War. On their return the delegates announced in the *Kazak* that the whole question had been dropped for the time being. Tynyshpaev asserts that nevertheless the whole question was discussed actively in the *Kazak* right up till the time of the announcement of the supreme command. The whole question, at least in the minds of the Alash Orda Kazakhs, was tied to the agrarian conditions existing among their people. Bukeikhanov and the others had gone to Petrograd with the goal of "bringing to the attention of the Government and the Duma the general opinion of the Kazakh nation concerning the future call" for workers while this general opinion consisted of this—that "in the event of an ineluctable call—to be placed in the cavalry and not the infantry with an equalization of the Kazakhs with the Russian Cossacks in land utilization."[11] In other words, the Alash Orda wanted the Kazakhs formed into Cossack communities with all the perquisites of that status.

The statement of Tynyshpaev that the Kirghiz and Kazakh people regarded military service as a welcome phenomenon in their lives, especially as with service in the cavalry they would secure land,[12] must

9. Deposition of the engineer Tynyshpaev, *Vosstanie 1916 g.v Kirgizstane*, p. 142.

10. Alikhan Bukeikhanov—member of the First Imperial Duma from Semipalatinsk, collaborator on the *Kazak* from 1912, commissar for the Turgai oblast under the Provisional Government. In 1917 elected head of the provisional Kazakh government, Alash Orda, 1917–1918.

11. Brainin and Shafiro, op. cit., p. 38.

12. Deposition of Tynyshpaev, *Vosstanie 1916 g.v Kirgizstane*, p. 143.

be accepted with reservation. The Kirghiz Kanaat Abukin mentions in his deposition the lively discussion that took place in the fall of 1915 regarding military service for the nomads but asserts that the general opinion expressed was to the effect that the Kirghiz and Kazakhs were unprepared for any such service as they did not know the Russian language or city life and that the whole plan for conscription was a figment of someone's imagination.[13] It was widely believed among both Sarts and nomads that the Russians had told them that they would never be subject to military duty when they first conquered the country.

The announcement of the order of conscription for workers, not soldiers, placed the Alash Orda group in a difficult position. While on the one hand they definitely did not want to see the Kirghiz and Kazakhs mobilized as workers, on the other hand they had pledged their support to the maintenance of the Tsarist Empire and furthermore they realized the utter futility of offering armed resistance to the very superior armament of the Russian forces. This group, after the announcement of the supreme order, decided to support the action of the government. Appeals were printed in the *Kazak* urging the fulfillment of the order by the people and the group was active in trying to calm the population and bring it around to the acceptance of the call for workers. The difficulties they encountered may be seen by quoting the experience of Tynyshpaev:

> I, myself, though personally understanding the essence of the whole matter of conscription found myself in a difficult position: at the gatherings of Kirghiz [Kazakhs] I explained that the term military work included work on the construction and operation of the railway, lading, the carrying of provisions, the guarding of horses, the chopping of trees for fuel, etc., but was sharply told that in the telegrams and newspapers nothing was said about this but only about emplacement work and that I do not speak accurately at all and that they had been told this by peasants they knew in the settlements, among whom there were relatives at the front.[14]

13. Deposition of Kanaat Abukin: ibid., p. 154.
14. Deposition of Tynyshpaev: ibid., 143.

These same peasants also repeated the usual stories that the natives would be forced to dig trenches under fire, between the German and the Russian forces.

Not all of the Kazakh intellectual class accepted the order with such good grace. The Astrakhan governor Sokolovsky in a telegram of July 20, 1916, mentions the activities of a certain Kulmanov, a Kazakh who had graduated from the university and had served as a member of the First and Second Imperial Dumas belonging to the Moslem faction. Kulmanov reportedly had collected a large sum of money from the Kazakhs and had gone to Petrograd to petition that the call be rescinded for them. He placed his hopes on the Moslem fraction of the Fourth Duma.[15] On July 25 Sokolovsky reported another delegation of three Kazakhs who had started out for Petrograd for the object of petitioning for the removal of the conscription order. All had served at some time or another as officials and all had been discharged from their posts for some reason not made clear.[16]

2. The Revolt in the Steppe Oblasts[17]

The announcement of the order caused the many Kazakhs employed by other rich Kazakhs, Russians, Russian and non-Russian merchants, Cossacks, and the Cossack army to abandon their work and to return to their auls, spreading panic there. Those Kazakhs neither employed by nor employing others also returned to their auls. The youths of subject age sold their property and brought a better horse or simply seized one from a neighbor. Gangs were formed of 50, 100, and even 1,000 armed with sticks, scythes, teeth from horse-rakes, and, in rare cases, hunting pieces. These bands of youths rode among the auls and gathered together their coevals with the object of offering resistance to the authorities. The hay remained uncut or, if cut, was

15. Telegram of the Astrakhan governor, July 20, 1916, “K istorii vosstaniya kirghiz v 1916 g.,” op. cit., p. 55.

16. Telegram of the Astrakhan governor, July 25, 1916, ibid., p. 56.

17. Excluding Semipalatinsk, which will be dealt with separately.

left on the ground to rot. The grain also was not harvested. In a word, the whole steppe was in an uproar.

The excesses of these bands were directed against their own officials, especially those aksakals, volost heads, and scribes who made up the lists. In some cases they contented themselves with merely seizing the lists; in others, they murdered the officials. When clashes occurred between natives and Russians it was usually in connection with attempts of the uezd head to protect the native officials and safeguard their lists from seizure by the dispatch of Cossacks.[18]

Disturbances among the Kazakhs are recorded at about the same time as they took place among the Sarts. Thus on July 8 a volost head was killed by the Kazakhs in the Uralsk uezd, followed by a clash between Kazakhs and Cossacks in the Lbishchensk uezd. Other outbursts are recorded for the Petropavlovsk and Turgai uezds. By the middle of July disorders were recorded not only in the Turgai oblast but also in the Temirsk and Uralsk uezds and several settlements of the Akmolinsk oblast. The end of July saw a great movement in the Bayan-aul region. Resistance took the specific forms of killing of native officials, burning their chancelleries, looting post offices, and skirmishes with army and Cossack detachments. Cases were even reported of the seizure of Russian women in the fields, tearing off their clothes and then leaving them to go home naked.[19]

It was in this setting that an informal meeting of the natives of the Turgai, Uralsk, Akmolinsk, Semipalatinsk and Semirechie oblasts took place on August 7, 1916, at Turgai with the permission of the Turgai oblast governor. The governor opened the meeting with a speech in which he explained the essence of the supreme command of June 25 and asked those present to help him in the work of the peaceful calling of the Kazakh and Kirghiz peoples. After proposing that those assembled elect a president the governor left the hall. The assembly elected as president A. Bukeikhanov and as secretaries M. J. Dulatov and O. Almasov.

18. Pamyatnaya zapiska o kirgizakh: "K istorii vosstaniya kirghiz v 1916 g.," op. cit., p. 67.
19. Shestakov, op. cit., p. 98.

After reviewing the circumstances under which the call was made and their consequences the assembly recommended that the mobilization proceed on the basis of (1) the proper preparation of the population, (2) partial mobilization in the course of a more or less extended period of time in keeping with the need, (3) the application of exemptions necessary for the preservation of the interests of individual Kazakh households, (4) the participation of representatives from the population so that the calling up of workers from the Kazakh population would go more smoothly.[20] In pin-pointing these general recommendations the assembly called for the postponement of the call of workers until January 1, 1917 (for the southern uezd, until March 15, 1917); to call initially one-third of the 19–31 age group, preferring the younger age group because among them there were the greatest number without families; allowing persons to appear for work either at the place of registration or where they were living; to leave in each family at least one worker; to leave those called up to work at home on government defense as far as possible (instead of going to the war areas); to give those taken the right to replace themselves with someone else; to leave one mullah for each aul community; to leave a teacher for every 50 kibitkas for the instruction of the children; to exempt the Moslem teachers in the medressehs in the cities; the old lists, made up hurriedly and incorrectly, to be replaced by new lists made up by a committee of representatives chosen at the rate of one for every ten households. The new lists were then made up in the presence of an aul assembly; two representatives for every volost must represent the native people with the right of vote; the further selection of officials in view of their malpractices to be suspended until after the call for workers had been filled; the workers to be given the right to form artels or cooperatives of 30 persons, each artel to have one translator and every ten artels a mullah; sick workers to be provided with medical facilities on the same basis as Russians wounded at the front; the Kirghiz and

20. Protocol of the informal meeting of Kirghiz, "K istorii vosstaniya kirghiz v 1916 g.," op. cit., p. 58.

Kazakh workers to participate in the city and zemsky institutions; free wagons to be provided to the workers for the transport of food and clothing; and, finally, leave passes to be provided for workers in case of necessity. The final article proposed petitioning the government to put these in force.[21]

Whether the government satisfied any of these requests is unknown. They have been cited *in extenso* as they show the mind of the part of the population which wanted to support the government in its call for workers. The provisions relating to the substitution of workers and the exemption of religious teachers testify to the class interests of those present in the assembly.

The disorders continued throughout August. The local authorities of the Akmolinsk oblast sent the following communication to Petrograd on August 21: "The Kirghiz [Kazakhs] are acting in a very provocatory manner, ride about only in large parties *and threaten the population of the Russian settlements that they will kill and burn in all directions, especially the very new settlements*. The Russians cannot defend themselves as the men of the Russian settlements have been taken away for the war. The Kirghiz [Kazakhs] attacked the Russians working in the fields, and took away all their draught animals, machines, carts, and harnesses. . . . In place of the usual 25–40 kibitkas the Kirghiz [Kazakhs] began to group themselves into 300–400 kibitkas. The Kirghiz [Kazakhs] gathered into a group of 15,000 around Lake Kurgalajin."[22]

The call for workers finally was postponed until September 15 in order to give the natives a chance to gather their hay and crops. Thanks to this, conditions in the steppe became more peaceful but the end of September saw a recrudescence of the disorders once again assuming serious proportions. Punitive units were dispatched into the steppes and a cruel pacification was begun.

On October 25 the Kazakhs of Akmolinsk uezd went *en masse* into the Kenderlinsk forest tract where they "mercilessly" began to cut

21. Ibid., pp. 60–61.
22. Quoted by Shestakov, op. cit., p. 98. Emphasis added by Shestakov.

down the forest. Cossacks were sent against them. The Kazakhs, seeing the Cossacks, jumped on their horses and armed only with homemade spears, charged the Cossacks. Volleys fired by the Cossacks converted this charge into a *sauve qui peut*. Forty-two Kazakhs were killed and an unknown number wounded. The Cossacks in pursuit came upon another band of armed Kazakhs and 20 more were killed. The punitive units swept on, killing, burning auls, winter quarters, and encampments, and robbing Kazakh food transports. On November 17 again 50 Kazakhs were reported killed, then 28. A skirmish between soldiers and Kazakhs brought 20 deaths to the latter. On November 23, 35 Kazakhs were killed in the Akmolinsk region. Disorders here finally came to an end on November 30, 1916.[23]

The revolt among the Kazakhs of the steppe did not reach the great proportions or as savage an expression as elsewhere, especially among the Kirghiz of Semirechie or even the Kazakhs of Semipalatinsk. Several reasons may be assigned for the much milder resistance put up.

(1) The Kazakhs of the steppe had a much longer history of contact with the Russians with considerable fusing of the two cultures through marriage and contact. Many of the Kazakhs had adopted a sedentary existence and practiced agriculture interspersed among the Russians. The Kirghiz, on the other hand, had a much shorter period of contact with the Russians, inhabited remote and inaccessible localities, and furthermore, were considered less tolerant of the non-Moslem than the Kazakhs.[24] The Kazakhs had a long tradition of acting in concert with Russia against the enemies of Russia. On the basis of the charter of the Empress Anne in 1731 to Abul-khair, Khan of the Little Horde of Kazakhs, the latter agreed to defend the frontiers of the Russian Empire from external enemies. This charter was invoked in the same century when the Bashkir mutiny was put down. Napoleon was pursued from Moscow in 1812 by forces including Kazakhs, headed by Baizhazyk Kushukbaev, right to the gates of Paris. The conquest of Turkistan by Generals Chernyaev,

23. Ibid., p. 99.

24. O. Lattimore, *Pivot of Asia*, op. cit., p. 134.

Kaufman, and Skobelev was accomplished with the material assistance and personal participation of the Kazakhs, while Chernyaev and Skobelev were counted as Kazakh national heroes.[25]

This long association bore fruit in the revolt in that the Kazakhs fought much more "like gentlemen" than the Kirghiz and others. Writing of this difference Governor Folbaum of Semirechie was to say, "It is necessary to remark that while the steppe Kirghiz [Kazakhs] treated their victims mildly the Kara-Kirghiz [true Kirghiz], and especially the Dungans, showed striking cruelty to the defenseless Russians, inflicting torture before killing, gouging out eyes, cutting off ears, bosoms, etc., cutting children to pieces."[26]

(2) The absence of leadership. Unlike the Turkomans and Kirghiz, the steppe Kazakhs failed to produce a leader of any stature. An official report was to comment on this: "But what was noticed was that the Kirghiz [Kazakh] youth searched for a leader but did not find him, therefore the agitation took the character of disorganization not different from the usual friction caused by every new development in the national life. This did not comprise a sign of rebellion or of agitation with the aim of separation from Russia."[27]

(3) The great distance separating the steppe Kazakhs from the border. The steppe Kazakhs, as a whole, found it much more difficult to migrate to some foreign country, for this reason, than did the Turkomans and Semirechie Kazakhs and Kirghiz. It is not a coincidence that the sharpest expressions of revolt developed among the Turkomans and the Kirghiz situated nearest the borders of Persia and of China.

(4) The lack of armament. Evidence shows that the steppe insurgents were more poorly armed than the Kirghiz and especially the Turkomans. Their armament consisted of crude home-made spears, axes, etc. While many of the Kirghiz were similarly armed, there also were significant numbers with rifles.

25. Pamyatnaya zapiska o kirgizakh; "K istorii vosstaniya kirghiz v 1916 g.," op. cit., p. 67.

26. Report of General Folbaum to the Turkistan Governor-General, ibid., p. 73.

27. Pamyatnaya zapiska o kirgizakh: ibid., p. 66.

(5) The nature of the country. The steppe was an easier terrain for the operations of punitive units than the hilly, remote country of Kirghizia, not yet linked by railway with the rest of Turkistan, or the remote desert country of the Turkomans.

3. The Revolt in Semipalatinsk

The revolt of Kazakhs of Semipalatinsk took a more severe form than among the other Steppe oblasts though not approaching the revolt in Semirechie in intensity and range.

The announcement of the call to the native population by the Steppe Governor-General seems to have been made earlier than elsewhere. General Sukhomlinov announced this in an order of June 30, 1916, explaining that: "The requisition order does not call these persons [conscripted workers] as soldiers into the army but for work necessary for the army in return for pay and provisions from the Treasury."[28] Despite these assurances the Kazakhs became very much alarmed. Rumors were circulated that the Kazakhs were being taken as soldiers and were to be baptized. The Kazakhs were clearly in an ugly mood.

Disorders are first officially recorded on July 14 in the Ust Kamenogorsk and Zaisan uezds. July 16 finds the disorders in Zaisan growing. Volost heads were killed and the Kazakhs began to leave for Sinkiang. More serious was the situation in the Karkaralinsk uezd beginning August 7. When the order was first announced there the people began immediately to show signs of dissatisfaction. The city of Karkaralinsk witnessed the influx of many Kazakhs who spent their time hotly discussing the conscription order, plainly shunning the Russians. Some of the Kazakh intelligentsia tried to win the people over to the acceptance of the order with no results. With the murder of many officials the situation became so serious that the Governor of Semipalatinsk was forced to make a trip to Karkaralinsk to try to talk sense to the Kazakhs.

The trip, however, was a failure. The Kazakhs killed a volost head

28. Stepnyak, op. cit., p. 133.

and a scribe in the presence of the Governor and attacked a pristav. The Kazakhs abandoned the fields and went off into the steppe. The Russian population displayed great fear for their lives and sent many petitions to the government for help, painting the existing situation in dark tones. The military force in Karkaralinsk was small and had only 15 cartridges per man.

In the meantime the disorders had spread over all five uezds of the oblast. Three clashes with the Cossacks were recorded. The Governor issued the following order to the end of pacifying the population:

> I inform all the Kirghiz [Kazakh] population of the oblast that they are not called as soldiers by the Tsarist order—there are too many Russian soldiers without them; the Kirghiz [Kazakhs] are called to work in order to help the Russian people who are fighting. Whoever can carry out useful work here will be left here, while whoever has no useful work here must travel to work wherever the military authorities direct.[29]

The order goes on to enumerate a long list of categories of work considered useful for the war effort. They included workers on peasant, Cossack, and Treasury agricultural tracts; those engaged in government service or as officials; native volost officials and mullahs; postal workers and drivers; Treasury flock herders; factory employees engaged in defense work (including flour mills, leather and shoe factories, wool washing, etc.); employees of gold, coal, and manganese mines and at salt lakes; those working on steam-boats, barges, rafts, beacons, as stevedores, and at wharves; railway employees, those caring for the military herds; fuel and produce transport workers; and, finally, graduates of upper and middle educational schools and those presently studying there.

This order did little to quiet the agitation. The Kazakhs continued to attack and kill their volost officials when the latter made up conscription lists The grain and grass of the colonists were trampled down, peasant herds were seized, and the Kazakhs refused to gather the hay and grain of the colonists. Finally the Governor-General Su-

29. Ibid., p. 135.

khomlinov postponed the call until September 15, but the agitation and disorder did not abate.

By this time the authorities had had time to form Cossack punitive detachments. For the suppression of the disorders the Semipalatinsk and Akmolinsk administrators coordinated their efforts. The pacification and carrying out of the conscription order went ahead slowly. Thus from the third to the twentieth of August there appeared only 127 persons at the collecting stations. The forwarding of workers in a body did not take place until the beginning of 1917.

The other main centre of resistance was the Zaisan uezd. Here the flight to China began at an early date. On July 16 the uezd authorities tried to explain the order without much success. A petition for postponement of the call telegraphed by some of the Kirghiz on July 17 was successful and the call was postponed until September. The Kazakhs quieted with this but the end of September saw disorders break out again. One peasant official, Seleznev by name, decided to ask for another postponement until winter. This petition was telegraphed to the highest officials. The result this time was unfavorable; Seleznev was arrested. His deposition contains much that is of interest as to the effect of these troubled conditions on the people, both Kazakhs and Russians:

> The Kirghiz [Kazakhs] are faced with a serious predicament: the winter quarters are not prepared, property has been destroyed by the Russian colonists, the wells have not been cleared. The Kirghiz [Kazakhs] are faced with a catastrophe and so are the Russians.
>
> Bread appears as a regulator of price in general trade. With a rise in the price of bread the price of goods also goes up. The prices of goods began to go up with extraordinary rapidity: what cost 10–20 kopecks in the morning sold at night for 40–50 kopecks. Such a rise in price reflects severely upon the modest budget of the families of soldiers and reservists receiving a food allowance that did not suffice for the satisfying of food needs, and, as was consequently to be expected, in Zaisan there broke out disorders caused by soldiers' wives and ending in the destruction of the store of Erzin [a merchant]. After this, fearing the plundering by the soldiers' wives of all wares in general the Zaisan trading firms

> began sending their goods in a steady stream over the border to China and in the city of Zaisan there began a trade crisis unthinkable before the call of the Kirghiz [Kazakhs].[30]

The disorders in Zaisan uezd ended on January 10, 1917. January 15 was designated as the beginning date for the call-up of workers.

In the Tomsk gubernia the Kazakhs began agitating on July 27 in the Biisk uezd. In this case the Kazakhs sought to avoid the call for workers by fleeing to Mongolia with their herds. Troops were dispatched to prevent this emigration; these were met on the Mongol border by armed Mongols.[31] The rich Kazakhs usually did not join the movement but utilized this as a chance to buy wool cheaply from those leaving for Mongolia.

4. The Revolt in Semirechie

The area of the most developed and intense expression of resistance to the Russians coincided with that of the most intense colonization by the Russians. Semirechie contained 300,000 of the 500,000 Russians in Russian Central Asia.

The outbreak of the revolt presented many difficulties for the Russian authorities. The men of military age were at the front, as military exemption was given only to those born in Syr Darya, Ferghana, and Samarkand oblasts—the three basic oblasts of the Turkistan Governor-Generalship. The military needs of the war denuded the country of most of its garrisons; even the few left behind for garrison duty were not regular army men. The settlers had been issued Berdan army rifles to protect themselves against any revolt by the native peoples, but during the latter part of 1915 and the beginning of 1916 these had been collected to help satisfy the desperate needs of the front. These rifles—some 7,500 in number—were found to be practically useless owing to the poor care given them by the peasants. The Russian colonies were difficult to defend. They formed a series of settlements

30. Ibid., p. 143.
31. Shestakov, op. cit., p. 100.

mostly along the postal road to the city of Verny. The usual settlement was strung out in a line for 5–6 versts. Finally the natural features of the oblast—the steppe, deserts, almost impassable hills and gorges—created great difficulties for any punitive expedition.

The uprising of the Kazakhs and Kirghiz began with the beginning of August, much later than in the other oblasts of Turkistan.

Governor Folbaum of the Semirechie oblast early foresaw that revolt was inevitable in Semirechie and made suitable arrangements to meet it. In July he divided the oblast into 17 sections and over each section set a commander with troops. The troops in Verny were put on the *qui vive* to be able to rush to any trouble spot. Cossacks not on active service were mobilized. Folbaum saw clearly that flight would be attempted into China and so he dispatched a considerable part of his forces to the frontier. Both he and Kuropatkin determined where revolt was likely to occur. Passes and canyons through which the insurgents might pass were studied, and a plan was worked out to squeeze any possible insurgents into the narrow mountain passages where they could then be massacred.

The arrival of Kuropatkin in Turkistan brought a further elaboration of these preparations. On August 11, 1916, several days after disorders had broken out in Semirechie, Kuropatkin sent a most edifying telegram to Folbaum:

> I consider that the basic goal of your activities concerning the suppression of the Kirghiz disorders is consideration for the protection of the lives and property of the Russian population. To this end arm all the Russian population capable of bearing arms with the firearms and other weapons you have including axes and organize them into units of tens and hundreds. Place part of the armed population on horses. I authorize the formation of three sotnias [Cossack companies] of reserve troops and four sotnias of Cossack status. Leave the bulk of the sotnias at the places of formation.
>
> Secondly, organize in the cities and in all settlements near and distant defenses; do not allow the possibility of a sudden attack.
>
> Third, strengthen the measures against fires.
>
> Fourth, against the possibility of encirclement prepare the necessary amount of stores, secure water for the settlements and cities.

Fifth, in an attack by the Kirghiz inspire the most desperate resistance. Remember the example of the Uralsk sotnia of Serog [Cossack commander] struggling desperately with a horde of ten thousand. The number of Kirghiz armed with firearms is probably insignificant. Do not be satisfied with defense where you can go over to offensive tactics. An attack, especially at night, by brave fellows 30–50 years old, even on a great crowd, may give the most decisive results. It is necessary to create panic.

Sixth, maintain the postal and telegraphic ties, restore them where these are destroyed, and organize a horse post. Where possible do not stop any kind of field work in order that the harvest does not fail this year. Carry out where necessary the harvesting of Kirghiz fields abandoned by their owners, counting the collected harvest as Treasury stores.

Seventh, concerning the actions of punitive units, destroying the resisters and attackers, do not allow any unnecessary and therefore harmful cruelties against those who do not resist; do not allow robbery, under penalty of shooting, by our troops or by the Russian population. Guard closely all confiscated cattle, horses and property and regard it as the property of the Treasury.

Eighth, I authorize you to organize field courts with the units and in the cities.

Ninth, reinforce as much as possible the military forces with the uezd nachalniki and pristavs, entrust to them, where you find it necessary, the command and military forces for the suppression of disorders.

Tenth, maintain relations with the neighboring governors of all oblasts. Report, at your discretion, not less than two times a day.

Eleventh, take measures to utilize all *rod* and national differences among the native population of the oblast for the struggle with the agitators. Without doubt there are Kirghiz and communities loyal to us—direct them against the mutineers.

Twelfth, do not hamper, for the time being, the migration of Kirghiz into Chinese territory while you have not coped with the internal troubles.

Thirteenth, I am sending to you considerable reinforcements but before their arrival show great energy in your resistance and efficiency, both by yourself and all the Russian population.[32]

The effect of the supreme command upon the Kazakhs and Kirghiz of Semirechie was not dissimilar from that on their cousins in other

32. Taken from T. Ryskulov, *Vosstanie tuzemtsev v Srednei Azii v 1916 godu*, pp. 46–47. Quoted in *Vosstanie 1916 g.v Kirgizstane*, pp. 80–81.

oblasts. The same wild rumors were circulated about the real nature of the call. The native hired hands and "volunteers" working on the farms of the Russians left their work saying that they must go home as they soon would be going to war as soldiers and would have to arrange matters at home. In some cases the Russian soldiers' wives expressed dissatisfaction, while in the settlement of Samsonovka they went so far as to petition the authorities to make them return to work by force, asserting in addition that the Kirghiz were preparing a mutiny. Another circumstance calling the Kirghiz home was the fact that the volost authorities, in their manipulations of the lists of workers, placed those away at the top of the list since they had no opportunity to protest.[33]

As in the steppes there was a great demand for horses with which to flee. The price of horses at the Przhevalsk bazaar increased by three to five times.[34]

Actions to counteract any possibility of revolt were taken from several directions. The Alash Orda leader Tynyshpaev and the gubernia interpreter I. Dzainakov did all they could to explain the order to the people and urge them not to break the peace. They distributed the paper *Kazak* widely. The position the *Kazak* took was that while soldier status and service would be preferable, the Tsarist command was genuine and would have to be obeyed. The paper opined that if the natives obeyed the supreme order and did their work well they could then petition for service as soldiers.[35]

The authorities left no stone unturned in trying to win over the influential classes of the population. The Jarkent uezd head called the mullahs to his assistance. In his report he singles out the activities of a certain Khusainbek Yunusov. This mullah delivered pro-government speeches in the mosques, and propagandized the other mullahs basing his actions on the maxim of the Koran stating "Whoever is the ruler be he Moslem or unbeliever, the subjects must obey him."[36]

33. Broido, op. cit., p. 426.

34. Iz sudebnogo dela po Przhevalskomu raionu: *Vosstanie 1916 g.v Kirgizstane*, p. 32.

35. Brainin and Shafiro, op. cit., p. 44.

36. Ibid., p. 47.

The authorities also approached the bai class and assured them that they would be exempt from the call. This exemption was later confirmed in an order by General Kuropatkin. The uezd heads called meetings of volost authorities and the manaps and explained the order to them. They were told that the lists must be drawn up as that was the order. These meetings seemed to fulfill the desires of the governor and uezd heads, though one of the Dungan volost heads (Novo Nikolaevsk settlement) Bulgar Mogui stated he would not make up any list and rode away. (He was later put in chains and taken to Verny on orders of Folbaum.) Folbaum was to telegraph the Governor-General concerning one of these meetings, taking place in Verny uezd on July 22: "The old folk, moved to tears, kissed my boots and said that all would be done as I commanded."[37]

Folbaum also took steps to remove subversives and agitators from circulation. These were arrested for "instigations and disorders" and placed in jail. On July 17 alone the arrest of 34 Kazakhs was announced in three volosts of the Verny uezd.

Folbaum seems to have been satisfied with the fruits of his labors. On July 25 he was to telegraph the Governor-General: "The population of Verny, Pishpek, and Przhevalsk uezds acknowledged completely what is asked of them and are ready to fulfill the necessary order. In the Kopal, Lepsinsk, and Jarkent uezds the proximity of the Chinese frontier has brought some complications. . . . The population has jumped at the idea of flight."[38] The first to go to China were the Dungans, starting with July 14. They were followed by the Kirghiz and Kazakhs, in the volosts of Jarkent, Lepsinsk, and Kopal, nearest the Chinese frontier. This movement started on July 17.

The manaps and volost heads had not been home long from their meetings with the uezd heads before they came back to the uezd government saying that they feared for their lives. They had been threatened with death if they drew up lists of workers while many of the

37. Ibid., p. 45.
38. Miklashevsky, op. cit., p. 264.

piatidesyatniki had their seals taken away so that they could not seal any orders. Concerning malpractices, many of the manaps and volost heads began to see that the drawing up of lists of workers was too serious a matter to tamper with. The common people would endure many things but not this. It was advocated that the whole question be decided by calling out all the Kirghiz of draft age to a volost meeting where the lists could be made up by drawing lots with medical examination in view of all present. The volost authorities saw themselves in a dilemma. They were threatened with prosecution if they did not make up the lists, while the population threatened them with death if they did. In the case of the Przhevalsk uezd the native officials begged to be arrested and put into prison.[39] This proposition was refused. The manaps of the Pishpek uezd sent a telegram to General Folbaum asking that they be allowed to have all natives appear at the volost seat and decide the whole question by drawing lots and conducting medical examinations before the assembled natives. The telegram was sent on August 2–3 and the answer received on the 5th or 6th was in the negative. They then asked for protection, which was given them. Bodies of troops rode out with the volost heads. To many natives it appeared as though the Russians were backing the party in power in the volost against those out of power.

The first open resistance to the Russian authorities in Semirechie took place on August 3 in the eastern part of the Verny uezd in the valley of the river Yassy, where a band of Kirghiz subject to the call attacked the authorities sent to make up the lists, leaving one dead and three wounded. A Cossack unit was quickly dispatched and the volost made an example of. The movement, however, spread over most of the other volosts of Verny and through the Kastek pass reached the Kirghiz of the Pishpek uezd. On August 8 an attack was made on a post office near the station Dzhil Arik. On August 9–12 settlements near Tokmak were attacked and on August 13 the city of Tokmak itself was besieged by a great mass of Kirghiz numbered at 5,000. Messengers

39. *Vosstanie 1916 g.v Kirgizstane*, p. 31.

were dispatched in all directions not only to carry out agitation but to seek to coerce the vacillating Kirghiz to revolt. Unlike the other localities of the revolt, that in Semirechie early expressed itself in attacks upon the Russian colonies. A series of settlements were attacked and where successful the male population was killed while the women and girls were generally taken into captivity. The Russian settlement of Koltsovka was destroyed, of its population of 650, only 35 remained alive in captivity.

The revolt took on a general nature on August 10 when the Przhevalsk uezd and a part of the Jarkent uezd revolted. The uprising occupied all the banks of Issik Kul, the valley of the Karkara and Tekes rivers. Bands of insurgents armed with sticks, spears, and firearms fell on the farms, stations, and isolated hamlets all around Issik Kul and on the postal road to Verny. The population was murdered, women and girls taken prisoners, and the houses and other buildings burned. Others tried to flee from the avalanche, leaving behind property which was burned by the Kirghiz. The refugees made their way to the larger centres of population where the administration had already fashioned a militia organization. Many were killed on the road by the Dungans of the Mariinsk volost who revolted on August 10. This was repaid with usury by the furious Russians. Units were sent into Mariinsk where they exterminated the Dungans and destroyed their villages. The arrival of additional forces in Semirechie from outside on August 19–21 brought the real work of pacification to a start.

The Przhevalsk uezd saw by far the greatest number of killed Russian settlers, the other uezds suffering little by comparison. By November 1 the casualty figures for Semirechie listed 3 officers and 52 soldiers killed; wounded 41, missing 73. Two officials were killed and 12 civilian employees. The list for the population is quoted as: killed, 2,025 persons; missing, 1,088. The enormous loss in Russian lives as compared to the other oblasts is easily illustrated when we bear in mind that figures for all the oblasts give 2,094 people killed and 1,163 missing.

General Folbaum explained the reasons for the temporary success of the nomads in his official report thus: "For the Russian population and the administration especially the revolt of the Kara Kirghiz in the Przhevalsk uezd was unexpected owing to the insidious treachery of the influential leaders who, on the very eve of the revolt, gave assurances of full loyalty to the government."[40]

Of great importance in converting the passive resistance of the natives of Semirechie into an active one was an event which took place near Rybachev in the Przhevalsk uezd before the outbreak of the revolt. On the 6th or 7th of August a band of Kirghiz fell on a convoy of three or four soldiers accompanying a transport of arms and ammunition. Killing the soldiers, they made off with the stores which included 200 rifles and 3,000 cartridges. The simple nomads were blinded by what seemed to them an inexhaustible supply of armament, being wholly unaccustomed to seeing such a cache of arms. These arms were dispatched to other groups of Kirghiz and did much to stiffen their will to resist. It was this acquisition which, according to one witness, decided the Kirghiz to adopt an attitude of active resistance.[41]

One of the greatest actions of the Revolt of 1916 was the siege of Tokmak in Pishpek uezd starting on August 14. Estimates of the Kirghiz besieging the city vary from 4,000 to 5,000. The Kirghiz showed a great deal of organization in their operations. The force was divided into 28 units, each distinguished by a flag of a different color. The whole operation was under the command of an upper-class Kirghiz, Kanaat Abukin by name, while each volost had its own leader. But, apparently, he was only *primus inter pares*, the other leaders having equal rights with him as he himself later testified. This is proved by a document discovered by the Russians with the heading "command of the chief leaders of the Moslems" where his signature is on a par with the others.[42] The leaders were not armed except for Kanaat, who had

40. Report of Folbaum to Kuropatkin: "K istorii vosstaniya kirghiz v 1916 g.," op. cit., p. 70.

41. Deposition of the witness I. A. Pôtselnev, *Vosstanie 1916 g.v Kirgizstane*, p. 47.

42. Ibid., p. 163. Kanaat Abukin was a great manap who was illiterate and advanced in age. He was later betrayed to the Russian authorities by his own son. He died or was intentionally killed while in prison—the circumstances surrounding his death never have been satisfactorily explained.

a saber. In battle they rode in the rear of their units—all cavalry—and chased the skulkers forward. The flags of each unit served the purpose of keeping the units together and not mixing with the others.

As to general armament the force was partly equipped with rifles, which included Berdan army rifles, flintlocks, and matchlocks. The ammunition was not plentiful—about 10–15 rounds per man. The rest of the force was armed with spears and axes mounted on long poles.[43]

The Kirghiz employed one tactic which deserves mention. In order to disorganize the ranks of the defenders they first stampeded cattle into the town and then followed closely in their tracks.[44] They also utilized homemade cannon.

The Kirghiz surrounded Tokmak on all sides, even from that of the river Chu. After the arrival in Tokmak of additional Russian units with cannon (two batteries) and machine guns on August 30, the struggle took on an especially intensive character, the struggle beginning each morning and ending only at night. The Kirghiz attacked from all sides save the north where there was mud. The defenders of Tokmak barricaded the streets leading out of Tokmak at all ends. When the Kirghiz attacked in one direction and failed they quickly changed the direction of their attack.[45]

The great heroism of the Kirghiz in these encounters has not often been surpassed. Folbaum reports that on August 20 the attacks of the Kirghiz "were so furious that despite the machine gun fire mowing down whole rows they threw themselves into the attack three times."[46] An attack was also made upon the cannon themselves where the Kirghiz succeeded in getting within 20–30 *sazhen*[47] of them before they were shot down at point-blank range.

The arrival of the additional units and machine guns and cannon removed all chance of success in the taking of Tokmak. On August 22

43. Deposition of Jushak Mametbaev: *Vosstanie 1916 g.v Kirgizstane*, p. 62.
44. Brainin and Shafiro, op. cit., p. 60.
45. *Vosstanie 1916 g.v Kirgizstane*, p. 162.
46. Quoted by Brainin and Shafiro, op. cit., p. 60.
47. 1 sazhen = 7 feet.

the Kirghiz bowed to the inevitable and made their way into the hills surrounding the southern bank of Issik Kul.

A siege of lesser dimensions took place on August 9 when 5,000 insurgents attacked the settlement of Stolypin in the Kochkorka valley. The siege lasted two days and was successful. A quantity of arms were seized including some broken machine guns.

The revolt in Semirechie reached into the Syr Darya oblast where on August 11 agitation was begun among the Kirghiz of the eastern part of the Aulie-ata uezd, bordering on Semirechie oblast. By the end of August and the beginning of September this agitation was converted into open revolt. The Kirghiz made raids on postal stations and Russian settlements, killing peasants and destroying property. The settlement of Novo Troitskoe, located far from other Russian settlements on the border of Aulie-ata and Pishpek uezds, suffered especially. Forty of the inhabitants were killed, homesteads were burned, and most of the peasants' cattle driven off. The disorders ceased only on September 24 when a special punitive unit arrived.[48]

The Lepsinsk uezd of Semirechie oblast, settled by Kazakhs, remained comparatively quiet throughout the revolt except for a few volosts. Here there were no Russians killed and no attacks made on Russian settlements. According to the report of Tynyshpaev to Kuropatkin[49] the troubles that took place here were due entirely to the abuses and machinations of certain of the native administration. His account of what happened may be summarized in the following manner: Many volost authorities in the uezd understood that the conscription order was too serious an affair to be involved in the usual party politics and began to draw up the lists of workers on the basis of justice and fairness. A few of the volost authorities, however, could not let such a favorable opportunity pass for making new exactions on the people. In the Makanchi-Sadyrovsk volost Kasym Jakambaev, the volost head and his associates, the native judge Okysh Omarov, and

48. Report of Kuropatkin to Nicholas II, "Vosstanie 1916 g.v Srednei Azii," op. cit., p. 68.

49. "Report of the Governor-General": *Vosstanie 1916 g.v Kirgizstane*, pp. 76–77.

Jeksembek Knyazez, began to demand money and cattle from the Kazakhs of their volost, promising that if they gave these they would be freed from the call for workers. Some gave, not sparing their property, while others refused.

To revenge himself on the latter Jakambaev reported to the Russian authorities that they were offering resistance to the government. Cossacks and soldiers were dispatched. Ninety Kazakhs were killed in one incident where the Cossacks fell upon an assembly of Kazakhs dissatisfied with the volost head and his associates. Numerous arrests were made, even of Kazakhs who had not been at the assembly. These were dispatched to the city of Lepsinsk, but before they reached their destination many were killed without just cause. This occurred when Kazakhs, tired from walking and needing rest or wishing to attend to their natural wants, stopped on the way. In two such incidents first twelve and then six persons were killed.

The power and development of the revolt in Semirechie was in a large measure due to the element of organization developed by the insurgents. Banners and metal emblems on the caps of some of the insurgents served to distinguish them. In the hills, workshops were set up for the preparation of powder and the forging of weapons. The insurgents had a well-developed system of scouting, and visual signals were employed to warn of the approach of Russian units.[50] The insurgents also strove to break means of communication between the cities and the settlements. Roads, bridges, telegraph lines were destroyed.[51] The Kirghiz were especially successful in their efforts to isolate Przhevalsk and its vicinity from communication with the outside. For a long time nothing was known of what was happening here and it was only with the arrival of punitive units from Verny and Jarkent, August 15 to September 1, that news began to be received concerning the situation.

The great centres of the revolt in Semirechie were the mountainous southern part of the Pishpek uezd, all of the Przhevalsk uezd, and

50. Kuropatkin to Nicholas II, "Vosstanie 1916 g.v Srednei Azii," op. cit., p. 69.
51. Shestakov, op. cit., p. 100.

the southern part of the Jarkent uezd adjoining Przhevalsk uezd. Here almost all of the Russian settlements were destroyed.[52] The survivors fled to the hills of Pishpek and Przhevalsk or flocked to the city of Tokmak. The Kirghiz and Kazakh population in the other localities of Semirechie for the most part remained peaceful and fulfilled the demands of the administration not only for workers but for yurts and horses for the army. Even in the areas of open revolt not all of the population was disposed to oppose the Russians. In his report to Kuropatkin General Folbaum writes: "Fortunately not all of the population of the revolting volosts were hostile in disposition; among them there was no agreement: the usual party quarrels continued. The active elements often by force brought the vacillating to adhere to the rebellion."[53]

The success of the Kirghiz in Przhevalsk was due in part to the personal inadequacies of many of the Russians there. Speaking of the situation in Przhevalsk city and its environs at the beginning of the revolt one witness asserts, "Some of the men were very cowardly and hid from the fulfilment of defense duty. To our shame many base cowards were found even among the intellectuals."[54] The witness goes on to attribute to this the killing of many Russians in the neighboring villages and the destruction of the villages. "The Przhevalsk agricultural school in my opinion also owes its destruction in part to the cowardliness of some representatives of the Przhevalsk intelligentsia and in part to the routine and procrastination which reigned in the Przhevalsk military council directed by the old and half-deaf General Korolkov."[55]

General Folbaum organized militias in the cities and villages and sent what detachments he could against the insurgents. These forces were quite insufficient and Folbaum asked for rather large additional

52. In the Przhevalsk uezd only two settlements came out unscathed. Report of Stefanovich. *Vosstanie 1916 g.v Kirgizstane*, p. 113.

53. Report of Folbaum to the Governor-General, "K istorii vosstaniya kirghiz," op. cit., p. 73.

54. Deposition of I. A. Potselnev: *Vosstanie 1916 g.v Kirgizstane*, p. 45.

55. Ibid., p. 45.

quantities of troops. The dispatch of troops to Semirechie was begun on August 9 when Lt. Col. Geitsig was sent from Tashkent in command of a force made up of two companies of infantry, two batteries, a sotnia of Cossacks, four machine guns, and telegraph, telephone, and sapper detachments. Another force was dispatched in a few more days, composed of four companies of riflemen, one sotnia of Cossacks, a sapper detachment, and 160 mounted scouts. Still more troops together with four machine guns and two pieces of mountain artillery were sent on August 17, and on August 23 Tashkent sent an arms shipment of 2,000 rifles.[56]

These troops were drawn not only from Siberia and the other oblasts of Central Asia; from the front there were dispatched two Cossack regiments with batteries of artillery and two Colt machine gun detachments, one of the regiments coming via Chimkent and the other via Semipalatinsk.

The routes taken by the other detachments were via three directions: (1) from the direction of Andijan to the Narin stronghold; (2) from the side of Chernyaev (Chimkent) along the postal route to Pishpek and Tokmak, and (3) the roundabout way by railway to Semipalatinsk and from there by march to Sergiopol, Lepsinsk, and Verny.[57]

The hopelessness of the position of the weakly armed Kirghiz in the face of such a growing preponderance of strength may well be illustrated by the telegram sent by Kuropatkin to Folbaum on August 21: "Together with the units you have formed, with the arrival of reinforcements directed to you, not including two Cossack regiments and a horse battery, you will have at your disposition 35 companies, 24 sotnias, 240 mounted scouts, 16 cannon, and 47 machine guns. Chernyaev, Romanovsky, Kaufman, and Skobelev conquered the oblasts of Syr Darya, Samarkand, and Ferghana with fewer forces."[58]

The weakly armed insurgents naturally could not make a successful

56. Brainin and Shafiro, op. cit., pp. 61–62.

57. Introduction: *Vosstanie 1916 g.v Kirgizstane*, p. 9.

58. Brainin and Shafiro, op. cit., p. 62.

stand against such a force and therefore it is not surprising that by September 1 resistance was offered only by small bands of partisans in remote and isolated localities. These partisans tore up the telegraph (between Pishpek and Verny), attacked small detachments, made raids on the railway and on Russian settlements. The majority of the insurgents, however, fled into the hills while some fled to China. By the end of September the revolt may be considered to have been liquidated except for the Zaisan and Jarkent areas, which were to keep up the fight into 1917, and for groups of *basmachi*.[59]

In the pacification of the country the Russian forces showed the utmost cruelty. Entire villages were levelled by artillery fire while against the insurgents themselves Kuropatkin gave the order "not to spare the cartridges." The nature of the pacification may be judged by citing a few reports. Thus one Russian detachment operating on the southern bank of Issik Kul killed 1,000 persons and took away most of the nomads' cattle. General Pokrovsky reports he "burned an encampment of around 1,000 yurts" while another general, Berg, reported that he exterminated "800 desperate Kirghiz warriors," besides driving off a great quantity of cattle and sheep. The Russian soldiers brought little credit upon themselves in suppressing the revolt. Kuropatkin complained in his journal: "Already during the pacification of the disorders in the Jizak uezd there were justifiable complaints against the army for the useless destruction of native dwellings, robbery, useless killings. This is also taking place in the operations in Semirechie."[60] The troops were not regular soldiers for the most part but made up of reservists and conscripts. The forces were little disciplined and coordinated.

One of Folbaum's basic lines of action against the insurgents—from the earliest days of the revolt—was the systematic seizure of their

59. Etymologically this word comes from the Turkish verb "to oppress," "press," "violate," and hence in Turkistan came to mean "bandit," "robber," "violator." In the struggle with Tsarism 1916–1917 and especially in the fight against Bolshevism in Russian Turkistan the word lost its pejorative quality and came to signify a nationalist rebel. See article by Mustapha Chokaieff, "The Basmatchi Movement in Turkestan," *Asiatic Review*, vol. XXIV (Apr. 1928), pp. 273–288.

60. Journal of Kuropatkin: "Vosstanie 1916 g.v Srednei Azii," op. cit., p. 50.

herds in an effort to undermine their economy and render them less capable of offering resistance. This seizure of herds reached huge proportions, as may be gathered from one report of Folbaum to Kuropatkin: "in the vicinity of Przhevalsk there were brought together over three hundred thousand head of cattle, in that of Kochkorka . . . around a hundred thousand . . . more moderate gain is still to be had in Tokmak . . . Further actions of the units will augment even more the quantity of cattle."[61] On September 3 Kuropatkin complained in his journal that Folbaum devoted more attention to rounding up the nomad insurgents' cattle than to rounding up the nomads themselves.[62] Finally even Folbaum came to see the difficulties created by his actions: "The cattle are being given to the administration but the latter is not able either to keep nor guard them without the help of the army, cattle may waste away and perish due to the lack of care and feed. But the troops tied to the herds lose their mobility."[63]

A great many innocent persons were killed during the suppression of the revolt; thus in the city of Przhevalsk 700 Kirghiz were killed who had in no way taken part in the revolt.[64] The indiscriminate handing out of arms to the Russian population brought very unfortunate results. Under the pretext of suppressing the insurgents, bands of Russian peasants rode about murdering and robbing without discrimination. Kuropatkin recognized this unfortunate state of affairs. "We must firmly establish that Lynch law on either side will be severely punished. Wantonness among the population is great. Sokolinsky [one of the Russian uezd officials] complains that he conciliates the Kirghiz and is accused of treachery. Everyone who defends the Kirghiz is accused of treachery. One must punish the Kirghiz severely but one must also firmly put an end to the Lynch law of the Russians otherwise normal life will not be restored . . . Many [of the Russians] are depraved to the core. Sokolinsky and the uezd nachalniks are of the opinion that

61. Shestakov, op. cit., p. 103.
62. Journal of Kuropatkin: "Vosstanie 1916 g.v Srednei Azii," op. cit., p. 50.
63. Shestakov, op. cit., p. 103.
64. *Vosstanie 1916 g.v Kirgizstane*, p. 161.

there are many disreputable, dissolute and even criminal elements among the Russian population."[65]

Even those natives who were arrested were not secure from the violence of the mob. A series of ugly incidents took place where the Russian population attacked these arrested persons under the very noses of the soldiers accompanying them or in the prisons where they were confined. According to a Colonel Ivanov: "Not rarely there were cases where the arrested did not even reach the yurts where I was situated; the crowd, mostly made up of women, threw itself on them the prisoners and obtained satisfaction in a very cruel manner. It was unthinkable to oppose such an action in view of the small number of soldiers I had at my disposal; it must also be taken into consideration that all these soldiers were local inhabitants, some of whom had lost their near ones or their property together with the peasants as a result of the revolt."[66] An especially horrible incident took place on August 13 in the village of Belovodsk when 517 arrested Kirghiz were brutally murdered while "trying to escape" by a savage mob of Russians without the least interference from the troops nearby.[67]

It is small wonder then that even the natives who had taken no part in the revolt sought refuge either in the hills or in flight to China from this whirlwind of violence and bestiality. The plight of those who fled into the mountains of Russian Central Asia was difficult indeed. The crops and winter dwellings abandoned by them were lost. While they preserved some of the property and cattle they brought with them, the absence of food for the cattle and the occurrence of drought in the spring of 1917 made their position extremely difficult. The fate of those who fled to China will now be considered.

65. Journal of Kuropatkin: "Vosstanie 1916 g.v Srednei Azii," op. cit., pp. 59–60. A Przhevalsk uezd police official asserted in his report that the "scum of European Russia" was sent to Semirechie. Miklashevsky, op. cit., p. 254.

66. Report of Colonel Ivanov to the vice-governor of the Semirechie oblast: *Vosstanie 1916 g.v Kirgizstane*, p. 38.

67. See ibid., pp. 163–164.

5. The Flight of the Insurgents to China

The first to flee to China after the announcement of the supreme command were the Dungans or Chinese Moslems. The Dungans in Russian Central Asia were settled for the most part in Semirechie, their largest settlements being situated not far from the cities of Karakol, Verny (Alma-Ata), and Pishpek (now Frunze). The special grievance of both the Dungans and the Uighurs was the so-called opium duty. While opium was cultivated by these peoples before the war in the Jarkent, Przhevalsky, and Pishpek uezds, this cultivation formed only a small part of their crops though an important cash crop. During the war, however, because of the need of this drug for the front, the Tsarist government forced them to cultivate the poppy seed exclusively and at prices that were very low; the buying of the crop was placed in the hands of the Treasury and all other sales were strictly forbidden, any infraction being prosecuted by the local administration and by specially constituted field courts. Wealthy Dungans did manage, however, to carry on a contraband trade with Western China.[68] The illegal influx of opium into Sinkiang was a problem for the Chinese authorities not only during the Tsarist regime but also during the Bolshevik Revolution.[69]

The first Dungans to cross the border did so about the middle of July in the direction of Aksu and Kulja. This was a party of those subject to the call and was made up of from 70 to 80 persons. The Dungans were aided in this by the fact that during their 40-year stay in Russia they had maintained trade and kinship relations with the main Dungan communities in Sinkiang, and thus they could avail themselves of these relations to hide from investigation and search. This was an important consideration in view of the fact that the Russians were in a strong position both legally and otherwise to demand the return of these refugees. The principle that refugees crossing the frontier either from the Chinese or Russian side should be returned by the other

68. Brainin and Shafiro, op. cit., p. 18.

69. Lt. Col. P. T. Etherton, *In the Heart of Asia* (London, 1925), p. 190.

party had been expressed with increasing vigour in the series of treaties between Russia and China beginning with the Treaty of Nerchinsk (1689). The Russian position, however, was strong not only *de jure* but *de facto*. Before the Revolution the Russians were strongly entrenched at Kashgar. The Russian Consul General "was usually a diplomat of high rank with an escort of a hundred Cossacks and a very considerable retinue. Owing to this and to the relative proximity of the Transcaspian centres of Russian culture, the Tsarist Consulate-General was the preponderating element in Kashgar society."[70]

The second batch of Dungans to cross the frontier came from the Przhevalsk uezd where they had joined the Kirghiz in revolt against the Russians. Their main centre, Mariinsk was, however, burned on August 13 by Russian forces and they were the first to lay down their arms and flee. According to one report the Dungans took part in the revolt in order to take advantage of the turmoil to take away opium to China.[71] What is certain is that a large group of Chinese merchants had gathered in Mariinsk at the time of the opium harvest when the revolt broke out. It is interesting to note that the Dungans outside of the Przhevalsk uezd not only took no part in the revolt on the side of the Kirghiz but even took part in the suppression on the side of the Russians.[72]

Dungans of this second wave first appeared in the city of Uch Turfan in Sinkiang on 15–16 August and numbered only several persons. This soon was increased to several thousand persons a day. This exodus also included Chinese subjects who had occupied themselves with trade and other professions in Russian territory. The Russian Consul General at Kashgar quickly dispatched the dragoman of the Consulate, Stefanovich, to Uch Turfan in order to take effective measures against this flight. The latter could do little, however, initially inasmuch as the Chinese could neither eject those who crossed the border nor prevent others from coming across. The great influx of Dungans

70. C. P. Skrine, op. cit., p. 66.
71. Iz sudebnogo dela po Przhevalskomu raionu: *Vosstanie 1916 g.v Kirgizstane*, p. 32.
72. Shestakov, op. cit., p. 100.

was completely unexpected by the Chinese and at the moment of the appearance of the refugees in Uch Turfan they had only 60–70 soldiers at that point. The most that could be done was to keep the refugees out of the city itself and to provide them with grain and provisions so that, exhausted by the rigours of the road, they would not create trouble.[73]

Refugee Kirghiz first appeared in Chinese territory in small numbers in the first days of September, The exodus from Russian territory was greatly increased by the latter part of September when the augmented Russian forces began a great drive against the insurgents. This migration was to last until the first part of November. Two routes were followed: (1) past Ft. Naryn through the Aksai valley to the passes of Turugart and Keltebuk in the upper reaches of the Kokshal river and (2) south from the city of Przhevalsk through the Bedel and Kaiche passes to the Uch Turfan and Aksu oases. The first route was impracticable for large groups. The proximity of Ft. Naryn served as a constant threat, the mountains are difficult to traverse, and there was an absence of pasture. The only Kirghiz who went via this route were those from the two nearest volosts who habitually migrated south from Naryn. The second route was followed by the mass of the insurgents. Good pasture was to be had all the way to the Russian frontier and the frontier was difficult to defend at this point.

The refugees from the Naryn region took the first route and were people who from the very first had little taste for the revolt. They fled from the Kirghiz insurgents themselves who, they were afraid, would either force them to join the rebellion or rob their herds.[74] In this case virtue triumphed and they were soon talked into returning to Russia, returning with their herds almost intact.

Far different was the fate of the refugees from the Przhevalsk and Pishpek uezds, most of whom had taken an active part in the uprising. These natives followed the second route to Uch Turfan and Aksu and numbered from 100,000 to 120,000 persons. Pursued by the Russian forces and loaded down with belongings, the difficult passes they

73. Report of the Russian Consul General: *Vosstanie 1916 g.v Kirgizstane*, p. 105.
74. Report of the Dragoman Stefanovich: ibid., p. 114.

encountered took a frightful toll of the large herds that they tried to drive with them. Along the Bedel pass alone over 10,000 head of cattle and horses were counted fallen by the wayside. One Russian official in Sinkiang estimated from the various sources of information at his disposal that these refugees from Przhevalsk and Pishpek uezds in their flight from the middle of September to the beginning of November lost almost all of the Russian cattle they had carried off. His figures are: horned cattle, none left; horses, 10 percent left; sheep, one-fourth left; camels, about one-half.[75] But at that the tribulations of the refugees had just begun.

The first period of relations between the Chinese authorities and the Russian officials was a good one from the standpoint of the latter, and lasted from the beginning of the revolt in the early part of August to the last ten days of September. The Chinese government in Sinkiang became alarmed at the influx of Dungans and other persons. Memories of the Dungan uprising of the 1870s against the Chinese were revived and moreover the Chinese noted that most of the later trouble in Sinkiang had been started by migrants from the former Kokand khanate. Ma-titai, the strong man of the Kashgar area at the time,[76] cooperated fully with the Russian authorities after the Russian Consul General pointed out the necessity to act against this influx of refugees. The troops at Uch Turfan were increased to 300–400 cavalry and infantry, sent from Aksu, Yarkand, and Kashgar. The Aksu *tao-t'ai* (chief official of a provincial district) Ch'u Jui-ch'i was sent to Uch Turfan where he remained for three months until the movement of refugees into Chinese territory had stopped. Stefanovich had already spent some time in Uch Turfan, having arrived there in July, before the disorders began. Stefanovich persuaded the tao-t'ai not to enter into any kind of relations with the envoys of the insurgents. The tao-t'ai posted guards at the frontier, not allowing the refugees to cross and at

75. Report of the Military starshina Bychkov: ibid., p. 103. The insurgents took along from five to seven animals per person.

76. *Titai* = commander in chief. For a fascinating account of this despot, and his demise, see C. P. Skrine, op. cit., pp. 85–89, 261–268.

the same time made it known throughout the hills that the insurgents would not be allowed to cross and that their petitions for Chinese citizenship could not be entertained. Petitions the tao-t'ai received from the refugees he handed over to Stefanovich, who took steps to persuade the refugees to return to Russia.

Oddly enough Stefanovich was most hampered in his efforts to repatriate the refugees by the actions of the Russian authorities and forces themselves in Semirechie. To quote from the report of the Russian Consul General: "but the measures of the latter [Stefanovich] to return the Kirghiz back to Russia, despite the desire for this on the part of the Kirghiz, did not attain its goal. By this time there had gathered in the Przhevalsk uezd a considerable mass of various troops and they pursued the insurgents so energetically that often they did not distinguish them from peaceful inhabitants. As a consequence of this, special messengers were sent by . . . Stefanovich to the uezd head in the city of Przhevalsk to ascertain the conditions for the return of the refugee Kirghiz, but these did not succeed in their mission inasmuch as the Cossacks rode about shooting at all who appeared on the road to Przhevalsk."[77]

The Kazakh refugees of the *rod* of Alban succeeded in negotiating with General Folbaum through the Uch Turfan authorities to allow them to return, but General Folbaum struck a hard bargain. He authorized the return of 17 volosts only on the condition that they deliver 1,000 horses to Przhevalsk so that the peasants there could use them to harvest their crops; that they send 3,000 of their best horses for the needs of the Russian army; that they give up all arms and all their leaders. If they fulfilled all these conditions they could return.

Until the last ten days of September the Russians had considerable success in their efforts to return the refugees home. The Russian Consul General at Kashgar, aided by the moral suasion of the Kashgar authorities, arranged successfully the return of the Kirghiz congregated in the area of the Keltebuk and Turugart passes. When Stepanovich

77. Report of the Russian Consul General: *Vosstanie 1916 g.v Kirgizstane*, p. 107.

left Uch Turfan on September 15, only about 20–30 families of Kirghiz remained in Chinese territory, these having arrived by the most difficult and inaccessible routes.

The Russian Consul General was forced to recall Stefanovich to replace Pozdolsky as secretary of the Consulate, as the latter had been appointed to a post in Kuanchentsi. With the departure of Stefanovich from Uch Turfan, and with no one to take his place, the situation rapidly deteriorated. A great flood of refugees was allowed to cross over the frontier by the Chinese authorities, who now felt a great deal more free in their relations with the refugees. This situation was utilized by the Chinese as an opportunity for expropriation on a colossal scale. The refugees were forced to leave their property, cattle, arms, and even wives and children with the Chinese authorities as a condition for being allowed to cross the border. Even the leaders of the revolt were allowed to cross; the Shabdan brothers, leaders of the revolt around Issik Kul, were allowed to cross with their herds on the payment of 35,000 roubles. Once across the border, the defenseless Kirghiz were harried by the attacks of the Kalmyks[78] in Sinkiang.

78. *Kalmyks*—These peoples form the western branch of the Mongols, living partly in Europe and partly in Asia. The Asian Kalmyks are grouped mainly in Chinese territory: in Kobdo and Jungaria, the eastern portion of the T'ien Shan, East Turkistan, the southern fringe of the Gobi Desert, the Koko-nor range, and in the province of Kansu. There are also Kalmyks in Asiatic Russia—near Kulja in the territory of Semirechie and in the Altai mountains. The European Kalmyks are widely separated from their brothers in Asia and are situated on the banks of the Volga around the cities of Astrakhan and Stavropol northwards, and in the steppes between the Volga and the Ural River. Before 1600 it is doubtful that there were any Kalmyks west of the Altai. A series of migrations into Asiatic Russia began around the year 1616 culminating in 1703 when the Kalmyks who had remained behind in Sinkiang resolved to escape from the persecution of the King of Jungaria. The Manchu Emperor extended an invitation to the Kalmyks to return after the re-establishment of Chinese control over Sinkiang after 1757. After one segment of the Kalmyks returned in 1771 large numbers of Kalmyks, dissatisfied with Russian rule, set out to do the same. The rigours of winter in addition to intensive attacks by the Kirghiz made this migration an extremely difficult one for the Kalmyks. Of the 169,000 who set out on the journey some 100,000 are said to have perished on the way. The Kalmyks, then, had ample historical justification for attacking the insurgent Kirghiz who made their way into China during the revolt of 1916.

Harried on all sides, the refugees in the Kulja regions of Sinkiang, hearing about the formation of the special all-Kirghiz uezd of Naryn by Kuropatkin in November[79] began to return to Russia. The return march of these refugees was frightful. In that year snow fell early and the passes were already covered when the Kirghiz crossed on their way back home. Most of the cattle they had left were lost on the way owing to lack of food. The people themselves died like flies from the cold, hunger, and the difficulty of the way. The old and the children were abandoned to their fate. Typhus and smallpox broke out, reducing their number even more. The entire line of march was strewn with bodies.

Those who finally reached home were literally almost naked. Their situation even then was extremely inauspicious. Their winter quarters were destroyed, the harvests they had abandoned were lost, the remaining yurts had been plundered or destroyed, their cattle lost and their goods taken by the Chinese authorities while they were in exile.

The Chinese authorities continued to show a non-cooperative attitude towards the Russian authorities. The Aksu tao-t'ai called the refugees his "guests" and said that any attempt to act against them would cause great agitation. The Dungans were reportedly sent to the Lob Nor region where they were given free land. Though the Russians sent a force of 60 Cossacks to Uch Turfan to seize the leaders of the Kirghiz, they managed to seize only 12 rank-and-file insurgents.

The situation of the Kirghiz and Kazakhs who remained in Sinkiang became ever more desperate. The influx of such a huge horde into Uch Turfan and Aksu sent prices of grain skyrocketing; whereas formerly Uch Turfan supplied Kashgar and other cities with grain, it was now finding it difficult to supply itself. Refugees with Russian roubles found the rate of exchange fallen to the equivalent in Chinese money of 25 kopecks per rouble. The price of cattle dropped while that of grain went up.

The refugees had a very difficult time staying alive through the winter. They had to sell their last belongings in order to live. The Uch Turfan bazaar was bloated with Kirghiz and Kazakh belongings—felts

79. To be dealt with in Chapter VI.

from yurts, kettles, lariats, saddles, household items. The refugees found it difficult to hire themselves out as laborers as the region not only had enough laborers of its own but a surplus, who were accustomed to go to Russia as seasonal workers.

Late in November or December the Aksu tao-t'ai was replaced by a certain Lu. This marked a new change in Chinese policy. At the first meeting between Lu and Stefanovich the question of the ejection of the refugees was first raised by Lu, who asked Stefanovich to petition the Turkistan Governor-General to receive the refugees back. This *volte face* was due to very understandable reasons. The Chinese were finding it difficult to supply the population with food owing to the great drain on food supplies and the high prices caused by the presence of the refugees. Scurvy and typhus had broken out among the refugees and were threatening the Chinese subjects also. In order to live, the desperate refugees turned to robbery and murder and disorder was becoming chronic. Most of the refugees were finally repatriated both from the Kulja and the Kashgar areas the following spring.

The refugees in their flight to China took along many Russian prisoners, mostly women and children. Stefanovich, when at Uch Turfan, worked to liberate these people when they crossed the frontier with their captors. This had an unfortunate effect in that the Kirghiz, hearing of this, killed their captives. When Stefanovich was relieved at Uch Turfan the Consul General sent trusted natives to the passes used by the refugees to persuade them both to return to Russia and to liberate their captives. Sir George Macartney, British Consul General at Kashgar at the time, describes seeing these people: "Well does the reviewer remember how later on a few Russian women, in rags and with shoes worn through, came into Kashgar, weary, emaciated, and diseased; they had been discarded by their captors, and had trudged on foot all the way from the mountains round about Uch Turfan, at last to find shelter in the Russian Consulate."[80]

80. G. Macartney, Review of Mustapha Chokaieff's book, "Chez les Soviets en Asie Centrale," *Journal of the Central Asian Society*, vol. XVI (1929), p. 102.

B. The Revolt of the Turkomans

Although the revolt among the Turkomans was longer in duration than even in Semirechie (starting on August 15 and ending only in the last days of December) it was not so sharp in character as in either Ferghana or Semirechie because of the special geographical position of Turkmenistan. Russian colonization in this region had not begun until after 1905 and was still too slight to cause the great resentment that existed in Semirechie and elsewhere. Even where disorder and revolt took place it was confined to two localities—the cotton-growing region of the oases of Merv and Tejend, and the herding area on the Persian border along the Atrek river. In the first, the movement was underground, breaking out sporadically in incidents but with no "open" revolt. In the second, there was open insurrection against the Russian authority.

The announcement of the supreme command was greeted peacefully by the Turkomans though individuals petitioned the head of the Merv uezd on July 9, 1916, for a replacement of this duty by a contribution of money or by being allowed to hire workers in their place.[81] The Turkomans, proud of their warrior tradition, looked down on work in the fields as degrading and were accustomed to hiring laborers from Persia and Afghanistan to do this for them. The cotton areas of Merv and Tejend were suffering from a shortage of workers, and the call for laborers, set for the end of July, threatened the cotton harvesting which was due to begin in August.

Opposition in the cotton-growing area was expressed in September and October by several attacks, mostly confined to Sarakhs and Tejend, on railway workers, watchmen, and the post office. The railway line was torn up between Ashkhabad and Tejend and a railway bridge was burned. There were no turbulent outbursts and no clashes with military forces. The subsequent announcement by the Tsarist government that the Turkomans would be called for guard duty and not as workers calmed down the Turkomans here. November saw the end of

81. Miklashevsky, op. cit., p. 250.

all agitation when 37 Turkomans were arrested in Sarakhs and the first echelon of native guards was dispatched. A movement of a similar sort took place among the Yomud Turkomans of the Khivan khanate.

The Yomud Turkomans situated along the Persian border proved much more difficult to deal with. These Yomuds had shown their rebellious disposition before when in 1912 and 1915 those subject to the Khivan khanate revolted. In 1915 an attack was organized against the city of Khiva and was beaten off only with the help of Russian troops under General Galkin. The activities of the punitive expedition under Galkin increased Yomud dissatisfaction even more.[82]

The Yomuds along the Persian border migrated each winter to Persia. In the second half of August large groups of Yomuds started to migrate to Persia earlier than usual, after refusing to provide workers for the war areas, and telegraph lines along the border were torn up in places. The migration continued to September when from the Krasnovodsk uezd there migrated 2,000 kibitkas of Yomuds. Units of troops with artillery and machine guns were sent against these migrants. Clashes occurred when Yomuds fired on Cossack patrols with Berdan and .30-caliber rifles. In September the fortress of Ak-kala was seized by the Turkomans. When a unit arrived from Ashkhabad to take the fort the Yomuds opened a strong fire against it, using dum-dum bullets. They were dislodged only after a two-hour bombardment during which many were killed, the remainder fleeing towards the Caspian.

Basing themselves behind the Persian frontier the Yomuds carried out a series of raids on Russian convoys and patrols. The audacity of these raids may be realized by describing one of them. On September 30 a Russian force of 250 soldiers, with three machine guns and two cannon, left Chat guarding a transport of food and other goods. This convoy was twice attacked by Yomuds armed with quick-firing modern rifles, killing Captain Pozharsky, and killing or wounding several of the officers and men.

From September 25 to 29 the Yomuds destroyed three Russian es-

82. Shestakov, op. cit., p. 109.

tates near the Gurgen river and attacked several Russian settlements. Of the latter four were destroyed and two partially destroyed. The inhabitants were successfully evacuated to neighboring settlements under the guard of Russian soldiers.

Sporadic fighting took place between the two sides all through October. Railway installations and stations were attacked, and herds of camels and cattle carried off. In the vicinity of Tejend there were attempts to damage sections of railway, bridges, and telegraph lines. On October 6 an attack was made on Tejend itself, but the Russians were forewarned and it was successfully repulsed.

When the native population near Sarakhs dispatched a party of guards the Yomuds tried to break it up but the group was safely dispatched to Tejend.

The month of November was marked by the same type of raids mentioned, but there was noticed a much larger grouping in the bands and the appearance of recognized leaders. A series of serious skirmishes took place November 1 at Chat, where the Yomuds suffered great losses though they succeeded in breaking telegraphic communication between Chat and Gumbet. Attacks were made on the fisheries on the Caspian Sea between Gumish-Tepe and Karasu but were repulsed by artillery fire and a landing from one of the Caspian Sea patrol boats. From the middle of November great bands of insurgents appeared near the Gurgen river valley. More clashes occurred between the insurgents and the Russians.

By the beginning of December a special expeditionary force had been organized under Lt. General Madritov. It was a very considerable force by European colonial standards, numbering 10,000 men, and including 6 battalions, 15 sotnias of Cossacks, 18 cannon, 17 machine guns, and automobiles. This force was landed at the Persian port of Karasu and the port was made a base of operations against the insurgents. The Russians were justified to some extent in operating on Persian territory inasmuch as not only did the Russian Yomuds operate from behind the Persian frontier but they were joined in these operations by their cousins, the Persian Yomuds.

General Madritov began his operations by retaking Ak-kala which had been occupied by the Yomuds. The western part of the Ashkhabad province was cleared, several leaders seized and a thousand rifles taken away.

The Russian strategy was to attack the insurgents from both the north and the south and thus squeeze them in the mountains from both sides. A unit under General Narbut pressed south from Kara-Kala towards Morava-Tepe. A great skirmish took place in the Segirim-Dagh pass on December 18 between the Yomuds and Narbut's men. The Turkomans numbered about 3,000 men, half of whom were armed with spears and sabers and the other half with various types of rifles. The bravery and courage of the Turkomans drew words of admiration from the Russian commander. The Turkomans were finally forced to yield and were pressed into the mountains. Meanwhile General Madritov's force was approaching from the south. The insurgents tried to save themselves by flight towards the west but were overcome by the pursuing troops in battles from 21 to 31 December. This signalized final defeat for the Yomuds. The leaders of the rebellious tribes were either seized or gave themselves up. In the final battles 3,200 camels and over 25,000 sheep were taken from the insurgents.

Though small bands were pursued by Cossacks throughout January the great mass of the insurgents made their peace with the Tsar and agreed to do all that was demanded of them. By January 20 there were seized from the Yomuds 2,433 rifles, 315 sabers, and 61 daggers.

In the north Cossack units operated against small groups of insurgents and "scattered" them.

The total losses of the Russian forces in suppressing the Turkomans were given as: killed, 2 officers and 50 soldiers, and a similar number wounded. The losses for the Turkomans are not given but must have been very much higher.[83]

83. Information about the revolt of the Turkomans is not plentiful and is to be found principally in the article by Shestakov, op. cit., pp. 106–112; the Journal of General Kuropatkin, and the Report of Kuropatkin to Nicholas II, "Vosstanie 1916 g.v Srednei Azii," op. cit.

6

The End of the Revolt

A. Group Participation in the Revolt of 1916

1. The Well-to-Do Groups

The term "well-to-do" members of the population included the great, middle, and petty merchants in the cities while in the auls and towns it meant the great landowners and cattle herders. The participation of these elements in the revolt was not uniform. In Semirechie, Transcaspia, and in the areas of the three basic oblasts well-to-do elements not only participated in the revolt but led it. These were the remnants of the old feudal order, the great landholders, herders, mullahs, leaders of the tribes. Those who did not participate belonged to the post-feudal times, to the capitalistic classes made up of traders, merchants, and usurers.

In Semirechie the manaps had sufficient reason to oppose the call. Ruling over the lives of the Kirghiz and Kazakh with an iron hand as volost authorities, they saw that now they must lose that control with the departure of the young men to the front. They realized that their rule was tolerated only because the people were ignorant and superstitious, seeing nothing apart from their hills and auls, and were apprehensive as to the maintenance of the *status quo* when these young men returned. They also realized that their party enemies were only too anxious to lead the people in revolt if they declined to do so. Thus the manaps were faced with the dilemma—"head the uprising and grab some easy plunder or cede to their opponents who wanted a general uprising of the people."[1] Moreover, as we have seen, many were faced with still another dilemma. If they drew up the lists of workers they were threatened with death, if they did not they were faced with prosecution by the Russian authorities. Thus in many localities they headed the revolt. Kanaat Abukin, one of the main leaders of the revolt, came from the manap class and had held several elective posts in the Abaildinsk volost of the Pishpek uezd. The Shabdan brothers were also members of the well-to-do class, their father having rendered great services to the Russians, under whom he had attained high office.

The situation in Transcaspia is not sufficiently clear though it seems that influential Turkomans headed the revolt. The names of two of the three main leaders certainly are significant—Shikhr-Khan Divedzhi and Essen-Khan. *Rod* ties appear to have still had much force and the kinship group acted as a unit.

The well-to-do classes of the cities in general stood against participation in the revolt. These classes were better educated, stood closer to the Russian population with whom they often had commercial ties, and realized the real strength of the Russians and their own people. They knew that an unarmed mass of people could offer no real resistance to a punitive force armed to the teeth with modern weapons. In the event of failure they realized that they would suffer through their pockets. This feeling of impotence was shared by other segments of the population in the great cities, they too standing closer to reality. It was for this reason that in some great cities like Samarkand no disorders of any kind occurred, while in others like Old Tashkent they were comparatively insignificant.

The well-to-do groups greeted the announcement of the supreme command with fawning servility. Delegations of "influential persons" met with Russian officials and assured them of their complete loyalty

1. Report of the Dragoman of the Kashgar Consulate Stefanovich, *Vosstanie 1916 g.v Kirgizstane*, pp. 111–112.

to the government, promised fulfillment of the order, made vows, and held solemn patriotic services. These obsequious demonstrations occurred especially after the outbreak of disorders. Thus on the day after the outbreak of disorders in Old Tashkent on July 11 a group of native officials and influential persons appeared before the Governor-General and assured him of their "complete submission."[2]

None of these delegations ever uttered any real protest to the authorities; at best in some cases they asked for a postponement of the order. When this was refused and they were told the order must be obeyed they accepted this reply without a murmur. Complete loyalty was sworn, prayers said, the Tsar's health toasted, and patriotic hymns sung.

On July 12 the influential persons of the city of Namangan at a meeting vowed "in honesty and frankness the wish for a victory of Russian arms."[3] On July 22 the Political Agent in Bukhara telegraphed the Governor-General: "There appeared before me today 20 of the greatest merchants, and inspired by feelings of genuine loyalty and love for Russia, they expressed their extreme displeasure concerning the rebellious actions of the Samarkandians"[4] (that is, the Jizak uprising). Similar sentiments of loyalty to Russia and displeasure with those who opposed the order were expressed in assembles in Chimkent, Osh Verny, Pskent, Margelan, Kokand, and other cities. Governor Kuropatkin during his tour of Turkistan records in his journal many demonstrations of loyalty to the administration.[5] Thus the well-to-do elements, in general, played the same part here as they did in the Andijan uprising of 1898.

The call for workers was disliked by the great class of rich money-lenders and they petitioned to have it replaced by a capitation tax. In the event of the success of such a petition they would have gained in three ways: (1) they would have kept themselves from being con-

2. Shestakov, op. cit., p. 92.

3. Miklashevsky, op. cit., p. 257.

4. Ibid., p. 257.

5. See Journal of Kuropatkin: "Vosstanie 1916 g.v Srednei Azii," op. cit., pp. 45–67.

scripted as laborers; (2) they would have kept under their thumbs the numerous class of peasantry owing them money; and (3) the need of the poor for money to pay the tax would have opened new horizons for their money-lending activities. Although the labor levy was not replaced by a pecuniary one, the Russian government in an effort to gain the support of the well-to-do members of the population issued an edict at the end of July allowing anyone drafted for service to hire someone to take his place.

The open support given by the well-to-do natives to the order alienated them from the common folk. This was noticed by the Russian administration itself. On July 22 the Andijan uezd head reported to the Governor of the Ferghana oblast: "the influential natives who used to exercise a great influence over the people have now lost that influence to such an extent that they openly fear even to speak to the people on the subject of the conscription of workers."[6]

The clergy appeared as a sizeable segment of the well-to-do section of the population. What explains their often active participation in the revolt, notably in the Jizak uprising? One element in this was the fear of losing their influence over the masses. The alienation of much of the youth to religion under the influences of some of the seamy sides of Russian civilization has already been mentioned. Presumably the clergy saw that if a great blow was not now struck for a return to the strict morality and pristine belief of another time the chance might not again present itself. Added to this the clergy had an exaggerated belief in their importance among their followers. Finally the element of fanaticism appeared in the background.

The religious influence on the revolt, however, must not be overestimated. If mullahs and other religious personages were involved leading the people in revolt, we find on the other side mullahs lending their prestige and authority to the service of the Russian state, the activities of some already having been noted. The mullahs and others were well

6. Miklashevsky, op. cit., p. 258.

represented in the delegations proclaiming their loyalty to the Russian government. The latter realized the usefulness of the mullahs and others and even gave bribes to secure their support. Thus in one secret telegram we find: "The Governor-General completely approves of the idea of using Ishan-Siakh to address appeals to the masses of followers in Ferghana and other oblasts of the krai. It might be made known to the Ishan that his loyal relation to our government's interests will not go unnoticed."[7]

The Okhrana was so busy on the eve of the revolt watching both the Jadids and the Pan-Islamists that the revolt caught the government by surprise. In the words of Galuzo, "The Okhrana had the same outlook on events in 1916 that it had at the end of the XIXth century. It seemed to the government that a movement must always appear under the same signs under which the gazavat was sounded in the Kokand khanate 'cut down the infidels.'"[8] The revolt caught both the Jadids and the Pan-Islamists by surprise and neither participated in the revolt, although the classes they represented did take part. Preoccupation with the details of the Andijan uprising of 1898 blinded the agents of the Okhrana to the new forces at work.

2. The Poor

Whereas no general picture is characteristic for the well-to-do native classes, it may be said of the poor that everywhere they participated in the revolt as insurgents. It was they who felt most keenly the land seizure, economic bondage, the bribe-taking of officials. It was this group, aided by the group intermediate between them and the well-to-do classes, that gave the measures of opposition their scope and intensity. At whom were their blows aimed? The table below compiled by P. Galuzo gives the answer.[9]

7. Shestakov, op. cit., p. 93.
8. Galuzo, op, cit., p. 156.
9. Introduction: "Vosstanie 1916 g.v Srednei Azii," op. cit., p. 43.

Persons Killed by Insurgents

	Native Admin.	Russian Admin.	Russian colonists, Cossacks, bourgeoisie
Semirechie	2	14	2,094
Syr Darya	7	3	45
Samarkand	12	3	83
Ferghana	34	1	—
Transcaspia	—	3	No figures
Total	55	24	2,222

Thus it will be seen that whereas among the nomads the main blow against the officialdom was struck at the Russian officials, scarcely killing any of their native officials, the converse was true among the settled population of the three basic oblasts. Ferghana, the most economically developed oblast, had the greatest number of native officials killed and the least number of Russians. The backward oblast of Semirechie had the greatest number of Russian officials killed, with almost no native officials killed. In the settled areas it was their own officials who were the nearest to the people and were the most accessible of their exploiters, making their exactions felt directly.

The table also shows that Russian colonists suffered the most where they competed most actively for land with the natives. This was in Semirechie and to a much lesser extent the Samarkand and Syr Darya oblasts.

A word needs be said about the general participation of women in the crowds during the demonstrations. In a country where the male was definitely the master in the house it is apparent that women were present in the crowd only by permission of their menfolk. The presence of many women in the crowds was a guarantee that Russian officials would be more disposed to talk and less disposed to order troops to disperse the crowd unceremoniously by force.[10]

As in the Andijan uprising, the poor had not developed their own

10. Miklashevsky, op. cit., p. 260.

leadership and were forced to follow leaders who came from other classes. Their demands were still weakly formulated and were directed against the immediate burden oppressing them—the call for the conscription of workers—though they showed their latent discontent and resentment by such acts as the killing of Russian railway workers.

B. The Question of Foreign Influence

The outbreak of disorders and revolt in Russian Central Asia seemed to be a golden opportunity for the enemies of Russia. The successful development of revolution here would divert much-needed troops from the Eastern Front and might very well touch off a powder-train that could change the whole course of the war. What were the responses to this opportunity of Turkey, of Afghanistan (which was on the brink of declaring war against Great Britain), and of Austria, Germany, and Bulgaria?

The reports of Okhrana agents from the beginning of the World War to the eve of the revolt have already been quoted to the effect that agents of Turkey and Germany and other powers were working very actively in Turkistan.[11] These reports continued the same theme throughout the revolt, while the papers were reporting rumors of the activities of enemy agents. General Folbaum, reporting on the causes of the revolt, cites as partly responsible "Propaganda penetrating from neighboring China (Kulja, Kashgar), where there are German agents and which has been spread by Chinese and Dungans arriving in great numbers in Karkara and Przhevalsk. Evidence has been found of the participation in the disorders in Semirechie of the Chinese anarchist party Ko Lao Hui, having a tie with German agents."[12]

Despite all these assertions an examination of the Okhrana files,

11. Great credence was attached to these reports by the British; see Great Britain Naval Staff, Naval Intelligence Division, *A Manual on the Turanians and Pan-Turanianism* (London, c. 1918), pp. 228–229, 231.

12. Report of Folbaum to Kuropatkin: K.A. 3, no. 16 (1926), p. 72. *Ko Lao Hui* (Elder Brethren Society): not "anarchist," but a Chinese secret society with peasant, soldier, and bandit ramifications and with Chinese nationalist, anti-Manchu traditions.

official reports of those who suppressed the revolt, and the depositions of witnesses reveals little in the way of concrete proof of the existence and work of such agents; nor was a systematic effort made by the various insurgent groups to obtain help from abroad. On the eve of the revolt the Russian authorities were informed that enquiries were being sent to Afghanistan and Persia whether help would be given in the event of an uprising. Enquiries were also made in Bukhara of the high ecclesiastics there as to whether a holy war should be proclaimed.[13] All these enquiries, however, were made in the name of various individuals, without the knowledge and backing of any groups and with no sort of general plan or tie-up. Certainly no help was received from these quarters, while the Bukharan authorities worked hard to keep the revolt from spreading to that khanate.

Speaking of the disorders in the steppe among the Kazakhs one report has this to say: "This agitation was not instigated from without, either by the Germans, Turks, or the Austro-Hungarians or Bulgars. If it had been instigated by the latter there would have been an attempt to get a leader for the Kirghiz [Kazakhs] either by paying out money or other means and to supply them with firearms."[14] Nazir Khoja, one of the leaders of the Jizak revolt, affirmed in his deposition that he received no support or encouragement either from Bukhara, Afghanistan, Germany, Turkey, or elsewhere[15] while Lt. Col. Dimitri Vodopyanov, one of the officers taking part in this affair, reported: "From my own observation and according to reports no foreigners were noticed among the insurgents. No foreigner of any kind was among those killed."[16]

Turkish Pan-Islamism failed completely in its mission in Central Asia as elsewhere. Lt. Col. Etherton, who succeeded Sir George Macartney as British Consul General at Kashgar in 1918 and who was a close

13. Miklashevsky, op. cit., p. 250.

14. Pamyatnaya zapiska o kirgizakh: "K istorii vosstaniya Kirghiz v 1916 g.," op. cit., p. 66.

15. "Dzhizakskoe vosstanie 1916 g.," op. cit., p. 69.

16. Ibid., p. 82.

student of Central Asian affairs, wrote in 1923: "After close study of the matter I find very little indication of the Mohammedans of Central Asia being influenced by the Pan-Islam cry; sympathy with Turkey was certainly not pronounced, and she is not regarded as the hub of the Islamic world. The politically independent factors of the movement are divided amongst themselves, and they would be apparent if it came to a question of definite organization and control."[17]

Placed in its international setting, the Jihad proclaimed by Turkey in 1914 was a failure as far as winning the war was concerned. The movements that took place against England, and to a much lesser extent France, by the Riffs, Egyptians, Persians, Indians, and Afghans did not occur until after the Armistice of 1918 and furthermore, seem to have been inspired not by the Pan-Islamic feeling aimed at by the Turkish Jihad but by the Western doctrines of "self-determination" and "the rights of small nations" used in the Allied propaganda war with the Entente Powers.[18]

Several reasons account for this failure. Prominent among these was the inner contradiction between the aims of the nationalism of the Young Turks and the internationalism of the Pan-Islamic movement. The end of the Hamidian regime had meant the end of Pan-Islamism, although the Salónica Congress of the Committee of Union and Progress of 1908 formally endorsed the movement. This was further complicated by the struggle taking place in Turkey between orientation towards Asia and orientation towards the West. On the one hand Turkey, threatened by European imperialism, sought refuge in Asia, looking towards its Turanian cousins for support. On the other hand, it sought to modernize (i.e., Westernize) the Turkish state.[19] The latter tendency was to triumph when Enver Pasha, the champion of Pan-Turanianism, was ousted and forced to flee after the Armistice of 1918 and when Turkey was stripped of her non-Turkish possessions,

17. Lt. Col. Etherton, "Central Asia: Its Rise as a Political and Economic Factor," *Journal of the Central Asian Society*, vol. X (1923), p. 91.

18. Toynbee and Kirkwood, op. cit., p. 56.

19. Kohn, op. cit., p. 244.

especially the Arab lands, and left a national state almost homogeneous in composition.

The Russo-Japanese war of 1904–1905 had also left its mark. This successful challenging of a great European power by an Asiatic one had had repercussions on the Islamic world so that an essentially defensive attitude was replaced by an offensive one. Henceforth appeals to force were more in evidence than appeals to faith. Another factor which muffled the appeal of Pan-Islamism was the irreconcilability between the aims of the incipient nationalism of the Turks and the scientific militarism of the German state. While Abdul Hamid had been able to use the German alliance for his own ends and to further his Pan-Islamic aims, the Young Turks were very definitely being taken in tow by the Germans and being made subservient to the *Drang nach Osten* of the latter.[20]

Still further in the background was the real lack of ties within the Islamic world or even within the Turanian part of it, save for an abstract acceptance of Mohammedanism. The Islamic world was split into Shiites and Sunnites and from this still further down into a bewildering variety of sects and beliefs, each jealous and antagonistic towards the other. Even in speech the Turanian world was far from uniform. Osmanli Turkish, corrupted by many accretions from the different languages of the Levant, was a far cry from that spoken by the other Turkic peoples. Ethnically the Turanian peoples were far apart. Central Asia, as we have already seen, had had a strong Iranian base since the earliest historical times. The Turkic strain in Turkey itself is quite small. History saw the super-imposition of a small Turkish warrior-elite over a non-Turkic population similar to the process that obtained in Bulgaria and Hungary.[21]

The conditions favoring the propagandization of the Islamic idea varied among the people of the Islamic world. In the words of one observer. "Morally, the common aims and interests of Islam have achieved some progress which, as is usually the case, can be traced to the influ-

20. George Young, "Pan-Islamism," *Encyclopedia of the Social Sciences*, vol. XI, p. 543.
21. Czaplicka, op. cit., p. 11.

ence of the Press but this applies only to the Turkish, Persian, and Arabic newspapers for in Central Asia the mullahs and priestly caste exercise considerable influence, and they have eliminated everything that is at variance with early conservatism, and newspapers and secular literature are regarded with disfavor. It is therefore only the Muslim Press, especially the Turkish and Persian, that has brought together distant parts of the Islamic world. In the present stage there is little in the movement, and the progress it has made in Central Asia and Western China may be regarded as negligible."[22]

If the Moslem peoples of Russian Central Asia received no support in their revolt in 1916 from neighboring Moslem countries, can the same be said of their brother Moslems within the Russian Empire, and did they manifest a feeling of unity with their Central Asian brethren? There were many factors bringing the 19 million Moslems of the Russian Empire together. A common religious faith and a common subjection to one centralized state were combined with a railway system which brought the different Moslem areas together (the Rostov-Baku, Transcaspian, and Orenburg-Tashkent railways). Moreover a system of economic reciprocity was being worked out between the different areas.

At the same time, however, many centrifugal tendencies were at work. The Moslems were widely scattered geographically. The Turkish-speaking Moslems (16 million) of Russia spoke widely varying groups of dialects so that the Osmanli Turkish spoken in Asia Minor differs widely from that spoken in Kazan.[23] There was a great difference in the duration of the ties of the various Moslem groups to Russia, the Tatars of Kazan and Astrakhan coming under Russian rule in the middle of the sixteenth century while others, like the Kirghiz, were not subjugated until the second half of the nineteenth century. The variety of cultures among the different groups was great indeed, running from

22. Etherton, "Central Asia," op. cit., p. 91.

23. It is significant that at the All-Russian Moslem Conference held in Moscow in May 1917, the official language was Russian as it was the only language all the delegates could understand. See Arnold J. Toynbee, "Islam in Russia since the Revolution," *Journal of the Central Asian Society*, vol. V (1918), p. 80.

the Kazan Tatars, living mostly in towns and engaged as professional and business men, and artisans developing a press and literature and engaging vigorously in Russian politics after 1905, to backward nomadic peoples like the Kirghiz. The variety of occupations was equally great extending from modern industrial capitalists to simple herders.[24]

In addition to the economic and historical forces making for differences between these peoples, the Russian government pursued policies aimed at keeping them apart. Thus though Moslems were allowed considerable local religious autonomy, no religious centre for all Russian Moslems was tolerated; separate centres for the Caucasus, Volga Tatars, etc. were created. Again, a differentiation was made in regard to military service, which was limited to the Moslems of the Volga Ural region, Siberia, and the Crimea.

One potential source of support for the insurgents remains yet to be mentioned—the many German and Austrian prisoners of war in Turkistan. From the early days of the war the Tsarist government had a predilection for sending large numbers of the captured enemy to Turkistan where ways of escape were few and very difficult. By 1916 the number of prisoners in Turkistan had risen to 190,000, most of whom had been captured in the fighting around the fortress of Przemyśl in Poland. In this number were included many "civil prisoners," that is, civilians living in that area who had been seized to prevent them from giving valuable information on the movements of Russian troops. It might be presumed that the native insurgents would attempt to contact these persons and induce them to take part in the revolt as not only were they the nationals of countries at war with the Tsarist government but also as they suffered terribly in many of the Russian camps.[25] Frightful epidemics, especially typhus, ravaged the camps unchecked. Despite these favorable conditions for enlisting the support of the prisoners of war, they appear to have played no part at all, though there may have

24. Ibid., pp. 74–79.

25. For a description of these camps by eyewitnesses see Capt. A. H. Brun, *Troublous Times: Experiences in Bolshevik Russia and Turkistan* (London, 1931); Gustav Krist, *Prisoner in the Forbidden Land* (London, 1938).

been isolated cases of participation. The single reference in the official documents mentions a Moslem being held in jail after proposing to Austro-Hungarian prisoners of war in the Saperny lager near Tashkent that they take part in the revolt.[26] Thus the prisoners of war appear to have had no influence on the revolt although escaped German and Austrian prisoners who fled to Iran were used by Count Kanitz, the German military attaché in Teheran, to provoke a revolt against the Allies in northern Persia.[27]

C. Measures Taken for the Securing of the Peace in the Future

1. Military Measures

A series of military measures were undertaken by General Kuropatkin to prevent any renewal of resistance by the population. Guards were placed near all railways, in cities and some settlements. In the Gurgen area in Turkoman territory and in Semirechie where it was difficult to send reinforcements quickly, sufficient forces were stationed to repulse in the main any flare-up.

Measures were taken to weaken the subdued insurgents economically. Thus in the Turkoman area Kuropatkin instructed General Madritov to take away all horses, and half of all cattle and kibitkas (nomad tents) from the insurgents. In the end he seized, together with 3,200 rifles, 780 horses, 4,800 camels, and 175,000 sheep, 2,500 head of cattle, and 500 yurts.[28] Similar exactions were made on the insurgents of Semirechie.

In view of the disorders in the Khivan khanate it was decided to strengthen Russian rule there. To that end Kuropatkin concluded an agreement with the Khivan khanate whereby a military agent and staff were established at Khiva.

Kuropatkin put an end to the double citizenship and residence of

26. Miklashevsky, op. cit., pp. 249–250.

27. George Lenczowski, *Russia and the West in Iran, 1918–1948: A Study in Big-Power Rivalry* (Ithaca, N.Y., 1949), p. 149.

28. Report of Kuropatkin to Nicholas II, "Vosstanie 1916 g.v Srednei Azii," op. cit., p. 90.

the Yomud Turkomans along the Persian frontier by the simple expedient of seizing the territory in Persia to which the Yomuds made their yearly migrations. A series of strong points were occupied by Russians including Gumbet-khauz and Ak-kala on the Gurgen river, while posts were erected at some of the passes. Thus not only did Russian forces operate over much of the Astrabad province of Persia in suppressing the revolt but remained in occupation of Persian territory after the revolt was suppressed. Kuropatkin recommended that this territory be formally annexed by Russia with the agreement of Great Britain.[29]

In regard to measures against the Kirghiz and Kazakhs in Semirechie, Kuropatkin was to write: "I have come to the conclusion that it is necessary, where possible, to separate these nationalities [from the Russians] for a long time."[30] To that end he called a meeting of officials in Verny on October 16, 1916, where it was decided to form an all-Russian area in the region of the Chu river valley and around Issik Kul. This new uezd comprised the area of the Przhevalsk uezd and parts of the Jarkent and Pishpek uezds. The insurgents from this area who had fled to China were not to be allowed back to their former territory but were to be settled in a new all-Kirghiz and Kazakh uezd in the Naryn region. In addition 200,000 Kirghiz who were living in the area of the future all-Russian uezd were to be forcibly ejected. The ground cleared was to be given to Russian settlers, among whom were to be formed five stanitsas of Cossacks. The whole project was to be accomplished in the shortest time, by March 1917. This exchange benefited only the Russians, who occupied all of the rich valley around Issik Kul while the Kirghiz were forced into the barren hills of the Naryn uezd.

Taking a leaf from the Andijan uprising of 1898 Kuropatkin followed the principle set down at that time that all land "where Russian blood was spilled" should be confiscated by the Russian government. This principle was followed in two areas: (1) in the Przhevalsk, Pishpek,

29. Persia, though nominally neutral, became part of the battleground in which the forces of Turkey, Germany, England, and Russia were engaged. See Maj. Gen. L. C. Dunsterville, *The Adventures of Dunsterforce* (London, 1920).

30. Journal of Kuropatkin, "Vosstanie 1916 g.v Srednei Azii," op. cit., p. 60.

and Jarkent uezds; (2) in the Jizak uezd. The fulfillment of this policy in the first area has already been discussed. In the Jizak area 2,000 dessiatines of land were seized, 800 dessiatines in the area between New and Old Jizak where Colonel Rukin was killed by a native mob, and the remainder in several areas where some 73 Russians were killed. It was announced that in the event of new disorders in addition to the punishment of those guilty more land would be taken away where Russians were killed. Kuropatkin was of the opinion that this would have a sobering effect upon the natives and hold back the vacillators.[31]

It will be remembered that a general fine of 300,000 roubles had been levied on the natives of the Ferghana oblast after the Andijan uprising of 1898. Kuropatkin decided to repeat this system of collective responsibility and began to plan the details of a future general fine. The assessment of this fine was only prevented by the outbreak of the February revolution and the overthrow of the Tsarist government.

Finally, Kuropatkin proceeded with the punishment of those taking an immediate part in the revolt. A mass of persons was brought before the court on the basis of unverified denunciations, but most of the accused did not admit their guilt. The accusations were of a general nature as not only was it difficult to specify precise allegations concerning the actions of the accused but the latter, besides denying their guilt, might question the competence of the courts and assert they were martyrs suffering for a just cause.[32]

The numerous death sentences and long prison terms were lightened by the Governor-General, presumably on orders of the central government. The death sentence was commuted in many cases to ten or four years at hard labor while a corresponding lightening of sentence was granted to many who had lesser terms. By February 1, 1917, 347 persons had been sentenced to death but in the end only 51 were executed. There were many appeals for mercy. Five hundred and five were sentenced either to prison or banishment.

31. Report of Kuropatkin to Nicholas II, "Vosstanie 1916 g.v Srednei Azii," op. cit., p. 87.
32. Miklashevsky, op. cit., p. 271.

2. Administrative Measures

Kuropatkin found that one of the basic deficiencies of the system of government was the extreme paucity of Russian officials leading to a totally inadequate supervision of the subject peoples. The uezd head, aided by two to three pristavs or police chiefs, could not adequately cope with all the problems of supervision with which he was faced. Some of the uezds among the sedentary population had populations of a half million persons. To the end of a closer supervision of the native population Kuropatkin added 15 administrative-police officials on a temporary basis. The increased expenses from the addition of these officers were met from the receipts of sales of cattle seized from the nomads. With the confirmation of these offices as part of the regular administrative system, the expenses were to be met from regular funds.

Kuropatkin struck at the abuse of the agrarian laws. He found that sales of land were made in clear defiance of the law, which stated that 6 tanaps of land must remain to each landholder so that he could not be stripped entirely of his land if he ran into hopeless debt. Measures were taken to enforce this law. Measures also were taken to ascertain the rights of the nomads to land left for their use, to their rights in securing fuel from forests, and for their protection against the encroachment of the Forest Service.

In the Merv uezd Kuropatkin found great abuses on the part of the Okhrana [secret police] agents. These agents had been carelessly recruited, even from among illiterate Turkomans, and since 1912 had distinguished themselves by their bungling and, in some cases, criminal activities. The agents settled accounts with their enemies by shutting them up in prison on the ground of political unreliability. Bribes were exacted to prevent the agents from carrying out their threats. Kuropatkin found many of the complaints against these agents to be founded on fact and released a number of persons they had placed in prison, at the same time imprisoning eight Okhrana agents.

Kuropatkin sought to remedy the previous mistake of not explaining sufficiently to the native population the essence of the supreme order. In his tour of all the oblasts of the Governor-Generalship, Kuropatkin addressed many meetings of native dignitaries and told them the circumstances and goals of the order.

Realizing the seriousness of the food problem brought about by drought and disorder General Kuropatkin took measures to have grain shipped in from Russia and Siberia at prices within reach of the poor strata of the population. It was estimated that 20 million puds were needed to tide Turkistan (including the khanate of Bukhara) over until the next harvest. Measures were taken to provide grain for the Kirghiz and Kazakhs returning from their flight to China, although Kuropatkin was faced with great difficulty here. Snow in the T'ien Shan, the lack of roads for wheeled vehicles to say nothing of railroad lines, and the great height of the passes made the transport of grain difficult. Despite this solicitude for the country's needs in food, Kuropatkin recognized that there still was a war to be won and took measures for the further export of cattle, horses, camels, and fish despite the fact that this might leave the native population lacking in these items.[33]

Finally, steps were taken to draw up a new polozhenie or law code for the country. This new code was to be in part a going back to conditions existing before 1887. The uezd head and other Russian officiais were once more to exercise supervision over the general welfare of the population. The uezd and oblast authority was to be strengthened by coordinating, through councils, the activities of the other departments of government with those of the uezd and oblast heads.

D. The Balance Sheet of Damage Suffered

The casualty list for the Russians during the Revolt of 1916 is officially given as 3,709 Russians dead or missing. Of this number 2,325 were killed and 1,384 were missing. The number of wounded was not determined as in many cases they were given attention by the *feldsher* or first aid man before casualties could be counted. The total of Russian

33. Report of Kuropatkin to Nicholas II, "Vosstanie 1916 g.v Srednei Azii," op. cit., p. 81.

officials killed was 24, and that of native officials was 55. The losses of the Russian troops were quite small: 97 were killed, 86 wounded, and 176 persons were missing.

The significance of the Revolt of 1916 may be partially appreciated by comparing the above figures with Russian losses during their conquest of Turkistan. The following table[34] gives these losses:

Regions Conquered	Russian Losses	Date of Conquest
Semirechie oblast	105 persons	1860–1864
Syr Darya plus Amu Darya division	744 "	1833–1866
Ferghana	134 "	1860–1868, 1875–1876
Samarkand	811 "	
Transcaspia	582 "	1873–1881

The above figures include not only the dead but the wounded also. Comparison of the figures for the conquest and the Revolt of 1916 shows that the rebellion cost the Russians more in blood than the entire conquest of the five oblasts of Turkistan!

The forces required by the Russians to suppress a revolt by natives untrained in military technique, undisciplined, and at best not having enough rifles to go around, without the assistance of railroads, automobiles, artillery, or machine guns was quite large by the usual standards of forces dealing with colonial peoples.[35] The Russians, in the suppression of the revolt, utilized 14½ battalions of troops, 33 sotnias of Cossacks, 42 cannon, and 69 machine guns. In addition such modern

34. Ibid., p. 86.

35. Thus, during the French conquest of Indo-China François Gamier with only 17 officers, 175 sailors, and 2 artillerymen took the city of Hanoi, which was defended by 7,000 men. See Gabriel Hanotaux (Editor), *Histoire de la Nation française* (tome VIII), *Histoire Militaire et Navale*, vol. II (Paris, 1927), p. 468. During the Sepoy Mutiny in India a force under Henry Havelock of a thousand British soldiers, 30 Sikhs, 20 volunteers, and 6 guns defeated a force of 5,000 natives on July 16, 1857. See H. H. Dodwell (Editor), *The Cambridge History of India*, vol. VI, *The Indian Empire 1858–1918* (New York and Cambridge, England, 1932).

aids as gunboats, automobiles, the telephone, and telegraph were also utilized. Even in the matter of rifles the Russians employed superior models in addition to having much larger numbers of them. Though the insurgents had some Berdans and other modern makes they were also dependent on flintlocks and matchlocks. They rarely had much in the way of cartridges or lead and powder to use with these rifles while the Russians, after the initial attack, sent in large stores of ammunition.

In a material way the Russians saw destroyed of their property 9,000 homesteads, large tracts of the railway, many bridges, schools, churches, and hospitals, stations, and other government buildings. The greatest material damage, as well as the greatest physical suffering, was in the Przhevalsk uezd, followed by parts of the Jarkent and Pishpek uezds. The Treasury suffered not only from the destruction of many of its installations but from the non-collection of taxes during the time of the revolt.

Great as the losses were for the Russian population they were slight compared to those suffered by the subject peoples, especially the Kirghiz and Kazakhs of Semirechie. In five of the uezds of Semirechie (excluding Kopal) the losses in population and property for the subject peoples are given below.[36]

	Kibitkas		Population		
Uezds	No.	Percent of whole	No.	Percent of whole	Cattle in percent
Jarkent	12,718	74	64,800	73	83
Przhevalsk	24,252	70	123,600	70	90
Lepsinsk	3,442	48	17,500	47	17
Verny	1,932	44	9,800	45	13
Pishpek	9,313	42	47,000	42	45

The figures for the oblast as a whole give a loss of 20% of the population, 50% of the horses, 39% of the cattle, 55% of the camels, 58%

36. A. A. Anson, "Vosstanie kazakov," *Sibirskaya Sovetskaya Entsiklopedia*, vol. I, p. 531.

of the sheep and goats. The area under crop was reduced by 163,000 hectares.[37]

The loss in life among the non-Russians of Semirechie has never been officially estimated though it certainly numbered several tens of thousands.

The economy of the subject population in Semirechie was dealt a blow from which it took years to recover. Here is the report of one observer who in 1919, three years after the revolt, passed through a portion of the area where some of the bitterest fighting took place:

> It took me nearly a whole day to drive from Tokmak to the village of Samsonovka. I kept passing large Russian settlements on the road . . . then Kirghiz villages completely ruined and razed literally to the ground—villages where, but three short years previously, there had been busy bazaars and farms surrounded with gardens and fields of luzerne. Now on every side a desert. It seemed incredible that it was possible in so short a time to wipe whole villages off the face of the earth, with their well-developed system of farming. It was with only the most attentive search that I could find the short stumps of their trees and remains of their irrigation canals.
>
> The destruction of the *aryks* or irrigation canals in this district quickly reduced a highly developed farming district into a desert and blotted out all traces of cultivation and settlement. Only in the water meadows and low-lying ground near the stream is any cultivation possible.[38]

Among the Sarts the greatest damage by far to the native population, both physically and materially, was caused in the Jizak uezd. According to official figures one Russian unit alone destroyed 24 villages completely, 11 villages from one-half to three-fourths, and 11 villages partially. The number of natives killed is given officially at 958 though Miklashevsky asserts that it was in reality probably around 5,000.[39]

The suppression of the rebellion did not at all mean an end to the suffering of the subject peoples at the hands of the Russian population,

37. A hectare = 2.471 acres.

38. Pavel S. Nazaroff, *Hunted through Central Asia* (Edinburgh and London, 1932), pp. 165–166.

39. Miklashevsky, op. cit., p. 272.

who took advantage of their abject condition. Thus one Moslem agent communicates the following to the Russian authorities on January 5, 1917. "The population has so suffered from the punitive units and is so frightened that not only is it afraid to talk of any sort of attack but even to think of one. All the difficulties which they now have to undergo with the railway workers and the guards (the theft of household goods and sheep, goats, and swine) they take without a murmur, not even making any complaints to the administrative officials, to avoid any sort of misunderstanding. . . . The former local bais in the village do not, at present, appear as bais but as destitute persons, ruined completely by the late disorders."[40] A similar mood of abjection and extensive marauding by the Russian population can be reported concerning the nomads.

E. The Dispatch of Workers to the Front

The first dispatch of workers to the front occurred in the three basic oblasts of Turkistan after the suppression of the revolt at the end of July. Among these workers there was a good percentage of "volunteers," often mentioned in the official reports and in the newspapers at the time. These in reality were workers who had been hired by others to take their places. Demonstrations of loyalty by these "volunteers" were organized by the Russian officials which took place at the same time that the punitive units were doing their work. A typical such demonstration was reported by the head of the Namangan garrison on July 25:

> There gathered around 1,000 native volunteers, registered for work, and having before them the portrait of the sovereign emperor, they went about the city on patriotic demonstrations, accompanied by prominent natives and crowds of people during which there took place the singing of patriotic songs and cries of "hurrah" in honor of the sovereign emperor and for the ruin of the enemy.
>
> They came to my home and asked that I come out and propose a toast to the health of the sovereign. There followed loud "hurrahs." The picture was imposing, those gathered begged me to be assured that they were gladly going to work

40. Ibid., pp. 272–273.

> at the call of the emperor. They spoke of their loyalty to the sovereign, assuring me that they will take every care to fulfill completely the conscription order.[41]

Thus these workers were utilized not only to take the place of the well-to-do members of the native population but also to take part in demonstrations instigated by the Russian authorities to whip up enthusiasm for the conscription order.

The dispatch of workers continued during the following months though the country was still in the throes of revolt in many places. On October 11 Kuropatkin notes in his journal that there had already been dispatched sixteen trains of workers and two train loads of Turkoman guards.[42] The end of October saw the beginning of the dispatch of workers from Semirechie.

Details are few regarding the provisions made for the equipping of the workers for their stay in a country strange to them. In the Aulie-ata uezd, according to the report of the uezd head, Colonel Kastalsky, to Kuropatkin, the cost was borne by a huge levy on the population of the uezd. Whereas the various taxes on the 50,000 kibitkas in the uezd amounted to 18 roubles per kibitka, per year, the special levy for the benefit of the 12,000 workers sent by the uezd amounted to an additional 100 roubles per kibitka, or 5 million roubles for the whole uezd. Over 100 roubles went towards the furnishing of clothes for each worker while the worker also received 300–400 roubles for himself.

By February 1, 110,000 workers had been sent. Of these 4,163 persons passed through Semipalatinsk to Omsk, 4,373 by the Central Asian railway to Krasnovodsk and on to Baku, while the bulk went via Tashkent by railroad to Orenburg. The dispatch of workers was halted for a time in February because of the severe cold, while the February Revolution at the end of the month was to bring an end to the dispatch of workers. On March 12 the commander of the armies of Turkistan ordered the sending of workers to be halted until further orders were received. Not long after this the Provisional Government at Petrograd

41. Ibid., p. 269.
42. Journal of Kuropatkin, "Vosstanie 1916 g.v Srednei Azii," op. cit., p. 57.

annulled the supreme command. The middle of 1917 brought the return of the conscripted workers home.

Part of the workers who were drafted were left in the Central Asian krai. By an order from Petrograd 10,000 workers were assigned to work in Turkistan on the railway and on defense work. In Semipalatinsk 2,000 workers were left in the country besides those classes already exempted by virtue of the fact that they were engaged in defense work, agricultural work, etc. Workers were also hired for the construction of the Murmansk railway.[43]

The workers sent to Russia proper worked not only behind the front lines but in the industrial regions of Central Russia, the Ukraine, etc. The first months of 1917 found significant groups of workers in Moscow, Petrograd, Odessa, Nizhni-Novgorod, Kharkov, and on the railways.

The workers in Russia found conditions most unfavorable. They lived either in barracks or under the open sky while their food and clothing were both unsatisfactory. At the front they were sent to dangerous sectors to work while those in the factories worked at the most menial and exhausting labor.[44] Their pay was most unsatisfactory—from 1 to 10 roubles per month. Because of their lack of good clothing and quarters they fell prey to many diseases. Those who were returned to their homes because of illness had little good to say about their experience. One Russian official in Kokand wrote in his official report in March 1917: "they [the workers] describe to the population all that they saw in rather dark tones. In the main they express dissatisfaction with the food and also they are unused to the cold climate of European Russia."[45]

The conditions existing among one group of natives are described by one officer detailed to make an inspection by the Asiatic section of the General Staff. This group of workers were located at the "Sortirovochny" station near Petrograd and were engaged in work under the

43. Stepnyak, op. cit., p. 139.
44. Brainin and Shafiro, op. cit., p. 96.
45. Miklashevsky, op. cit., p. 273.

direction of the motor vehicle division of the Army. Second Lieutenant Matveev, who made the inspection on March 23, 1917, placed the number of workers here at 1,300. He found most of the workers living in earthen barracks poorly suited for living purposes, especially for the natives accustomed to a southern climate. The remainder of the workers, some 200 in number, lived in railway sleeping cars. Matveev characterizes the conditions he found in the barracks as follows:

> The dampness, the odors from drying clothes and shoes, and the large number of people living in the barracks made the air unbearable. Here in addition there were found sick people, many of whom do not have the strength to get up. The presence of these sick persons is explained, according to one of the administrative personnel present there, by the lack of sufficient beds in the hospital and also by the great number of sick persons.[46]

Matveev then goes on to describe the conditions under which the workers quartered in the sleeping cars lived: "The conditions of the workers living in the sleeping cars from their very arrival and lasting through five severe winter months were even worse."[47]

The administration, Matveev complains, did nothing to better these conditions even though much improvement could have been made with only a limited expenditure of money. In the matter of food, conditions were equally unsatisfactory. "The wasted appearance of the majority of workers completely emphasizes the insufficiency of food."

Working conditions were no better. The work day started at seven o'clock in the morning and lasted until six o'clock at night, but inasmuch as the workers were required to travel from one to one and a half hours to reach their place of work they were forced to arise at from five to six o'clock in the morning. They worked seven days a week and Matveev reported that they had had only two holidays off in five months.

Upon arrival in the camp the workers were issued 12 to 15 short fur

46. Deposition of Lt. Matveev, "Iz istorii vosstaniya kirgizov i kazakov v 1916 g." *Borba Klassov*, no. 7–8 (1932), p. 138.

47. Ibid.

cloaks per hundred, 12 to 15 felt boots, and 50 gloves per hundred, and all were given a pair of underwear. Matveev found the workers needing shoes badly, which item had been in short supply for a long time.

In the matter of pay the natives expressed bewilderment as some were given more and some less in the matter of pay. Since most of the workers were illiterate they had no way to check the wage rates.

The workers had access to a bath but, inasmuch as this was open from nine in the morning to nine at night, the workers had only an hour to an hour and a half at the end of the day to avail themselves of this facility. The workers told Matveev that in all the time they were there they had taken a bath only three times.

Matveev then concludes his report with the complaint that the non-commissioned officers present resorted to physical force at times when dealing with the natives, that bribe-taking was prevalent, that complaints were suppressed, and that the Russian authorities deliberately minimized the authority of the officials elected by the natives from their ranks (the "thousanders").

F. The Duma and the Revolt

Not only the Tsarist government but also the Duma were greatly alarmed when information about the first disorders in Turkistan were reported. At the same time that Kuropatkin was appointed Governor-General, the Duma sent a special commission to Turkistan composed of the Duma members Alexander Kerensky and the representatives of the Moslem faction Tevkelev. On September 10 these members reported their findings to a closed meeting of members of the Duma. These findings were discussed during the latter part of September at meetings of the military commission of the State Duma. Finally at the beginning of December three questions were asked of the government in the Duma. In the drawing up of these questions there participated the Moslem, Menshevik, Cadet, and Progressive sections of the Duma. Before proceeding with the questions themselves the inquiry of the Duma noted that it had repeatedly pointed to the irregularity of the principle which exempted the natives of Central Asia and the Caucasus from military service. The natives now were being called for work behind the lines which was relatively safe in comparison with service at the front. The Duma also pointed out that this measure had been adopted without the participation of the Duma, the legal institution for dealing with such questions. The government, especially the Ministers of War and of the Interior, had showed an utter incapability of dealing with the situation which had arisen in Turkistan. They had initiated the call without any preliminary regulations being issued. The three questions themselves were as follows: (1) Did the Prime Minister and the Ministers of the Interior and of War know that in taking the natives for work in the rear without the participation of the Duma in the question they infringed on the basic laws of the country, and did they not know that in not promulgating detailed regulations for the call of workers they had not fulfilled the second point of the supreme command of June 25, 1915? (2) An inquiry is made of the Minister of Justice as to why he allowed the promulgation of the said irregular measures and did not afterwards institute a criminal investigation against the guilty persons. (3) If the above is known to the said ministers what measures have been taken to make right the violated provisions of the law?

The Duma never received satisfaction in its interrogation, and the whole incident shows the impotence of the Duma in the face of the actions of the Tsar's ministers. On the other hand, it was even more drastic in its demands than the Tsarist government in that it demanded military service for all subject peoples, and not work conscription as an alternative.

7

The Revolt in Retrospect

A. The Early Soviet Interpretation of the Revolt

The first interpretation which may be considered is that of G. I. Broido, which is confined only to the Kirghiz and Kazakh phases of the revolt. This first-hand observer does not see the immediate cause of the revolt, apart from the order for the conscription of workers, in the reaction of the Kirghiz to the encroachment of the Resettlement Administration and other government institutions upon their lands, though this despoliation was going along rapidly at this time.[1] The destruction and disorganization of the community through the policies

1. See Broido, op. cit., p. 434. *Grigorii Isaakovich Broido* (born 1885). In 1905 he joined the Bolshevik wing of the Social Democratic Party and carried on agitation among the soldiers, editing the newspaper *Soldatskaya Gazeta* (Soldiers' Newspaper) in Tashkent. Broido was suspected of having a part in fomenting the revolt in Semirechie in 1916 and was arrested soon after the disorders began on orders of the Ministry of War. He was sent to Kasalinsk to the 1st Siberian rifle battalion in whose prison he remained until the first days of the February revolution. Soon after his arrest he was questioned about the causes and circumstances of the outbreak of the revolt in Semirechie and this deposition is one of the basic sources used in the present study ("Materialy k istorii vosstaniya kirghiz v 1916 g.," *Novy Vostok*, No. 6 [1924]). Upon his release from prison after the overthrow of the Tsarist government Broido hurried to Tashkent where he became the head of the Tashkent Soviet of Workers and Soldiers' Deputies as a Menshevik which, together with the less radical "Turkistan Committee," made up of officials and supporters of the Provisional Government, ruled over much of Russian Central Asia. Both of these bodies were made up exclusively or almost exclusively of Russians, thereby excluding the local Moslem population.

of the Russian government, Broido argues, had reached such a degree by the time of the revolt that there was no opportunity for any sort of secret meeting or preparation for an uprising. Any attempt to plot any kind of action would have been immediately made known to the authorities through "their" Kirghiz. Nor could the cause of the uprising have been national or religious aspirations. These were much weaker among the Kirghiz than among the Uzbeks, among whom there was no general uprising. Nor could this have been a movement of opposition to the war inasmuch as the level of political development among the Kirghiz was still at a very low level and they had no comprehension as to why the war was being fought and what were the goals of each side. Moreover the Kirghiz had asked to be taken into the army on the same terms as the Russians. *In the view of Broido the uprising was deliberately provoked by the Russian administration, including the high officials of Tashkent and Verny, so that an excuse could be found to exterminate the Kirghiz and to seize their land.* The great seizures of land from the Kirghiz had reached such proportions that it was only by such means that more land could be taken away from them. The deliberateness of the provocation was manifested through such acts as the clumsy and provocatory nature of the orders issued, the false explanations of the officials, the wanton acts of the Russian settlers and their organization into military units, the unpunished mass murders. All this was calculated to provoke an uprising by the Kirghiz. Once the disorders were started they were only intensified by the actions of the police and the peasant militia, making the Kirghiz look more and more like enemies in the eyes of the army sent in to repress the revolt.

This view of Broido was seconded by T. Ryskulov in an article which does not give such a detailed elaboration of this assertion as does

---

Later Broido rejoined the Bolsheviks. In 1919 he became a member of the Revolutionary War Council of the 1st Army on the Eastern front. He took part in the organization of the Communist University of the Toilers of the East in Moscow and was its director until 1926. From 1921 to 1923 Broido was Assistant Commissar for National Affairs in the central government and from 1925 to 1927 he was director of the State Publishing Works. His works include: *Natsionalno-kolonialny vopros* (Moscow, 1924); *Natsionalny vopros i* VKP (b) (Moscow, 1925).

Broido,[2] though Ryskulov adds that this seized land would form a *place d'armes* for further penetration into Persia, China, and Afghanistan.

This theory of "provocation" is vigorously attacked by A. V. Shestakov in his article on the Revolt of 1916.[3] He points out that immigration in the war years was insignificant. The authorities in the mother country were faced with such serious agricultural, military, and political problems that to provoke an uprising in Central Asia would have been the height of folly. Shestakov further buttresses his argument by the following considerations: (1) In the period of classic capitalism there was no similar case of provocation in the colonies during a period of military collapse and complete military and economic disintegration in the mother country. (2) The "cotton imperialists" together with the Moscow Bourse demanded the quickest measures towards the securing of normal conditions in the cotton areas, inasmuch as at that time Turkistan was the single source of cotton and provocation would have had serious repercussions on the furnishing of adequate clothing to the army. (3) The landholders, in their search for more working hands, were recruiting "Yellow" workers from Mongolia and China, and seeking to utilize the prisoners of war and the refugees. While they sought the workers of Central Asia in addition they could have accomplished their goal by means other than the provocation of an uprising. (4) The uprising took place not only in the Kirghiz areas where herding was the dominant economic pursuit and where land seizure was at its height, but also in areas where agriculture was intensively carried on. Any sort of movement in the latter area would have menaced its economy. (5) To think that Kuropatkin, knowing the country of Turkistan well, would not have taken this into consideration would be the same mistake as to suppose that Kuropatkin did not foresee the range of the revolt.

Shestakov goes on to say that the number of troops in Turkistan when the revolt began was small. To think that a provocation would be started in Turkistan at a time when conditions at the front were so

2. T. Ryskulov, "Iz istorii borby za osvobozhdenie vostoka (vosstanie kirghiz Turkestana protiv tsarisma v 1916 g.)," *Novy vostok*, no. 6 (1924).

3. Shestakov, op. cit., pp. 84–86.

critical is senseless. Shestakov then goes on to criticize writers on the Revolt of 1916 in general, saying that they took the course and characteristics of actions occurring in one part of the country and made broad generalizations applying to the country as a whole without any regard for their differing social, cultural, and economic backgrounds. Broido, in his view, is especially guilty of this practice. He witnessed the goading into revolt of the peaceful Kirghiz of one part of the Semirechie and from that deduced that this provocation occurred in all the territory.

Shestakov himself sees the cause of the revolt in the opposition of the native peoples to the blood tax they were asked to pay by the Tsarist government. The talk of using them as laborers was pure camouflage. In this Turkistan differed in nothing from other colonial areas. The colonizing powers were not satisfied in looking to the colony as a source of raw materials, a market for their goods and an outlet for their surplus workers. The colony was also looked upon as a source of cannon fodder to be used in the wars of the mother country. Natives were used on the battlefield, as happened in 1914–1918, in occupied zones and as an instrument in suppressing the class struggle conducted by the workers and peasants.

Russia already had native units fighting for it at the front (such as the Turkoman regiment). The propensity of imperialist powers to utilize their natives as cannon fodder is brought out by the inquiry of the Duma, dealt with in the last chapter, in which the exemption from service of the natives of Central Asia and the Caucasus was attacked as an abnormality. The natives who offered resistance to the labor conscription well understood in Shestakov's view that this was in reality but the first step towards being converted into soldiers.

Brainin and Shafiro[4] discern the especial importance of the revolt in the fact that the workers sent to work in Russia proper came into contact with the revolutionary doctrines and workers of the Bolshevik party. Among the workers who were quickly brought over to the side of the Bolsheviks a prominent part was played by those who had actively

4. Brainin and Shafiro, op. cit., pp. 90–104.

participated in the Revolt of 1916. Their suppression had only inflamed them all the more against the Tsarist regime. While Kuropatkin in one of his orders at the end of 1916 expressed the opinion that the workers dispatched for work to Russia "will return to the homeland better off than before, having been acquainted with the might and greatness of the Russian State," in reality they returned in a bellicose frame of mind, many having become Bolsheviks in the meantime. They were to play a prominent part in the seizure of power by the Soviets according to Brainin and Shafiro.

The role of the manaps or aristocracy in the revolt among the Kazakhs and Kirghiz is a subject of no little controversy among the Soviet writers dealing with the subject. Miklashevsky and Shestakov assert that the manaps not only went along with the poor in the revolt but even led them. Brainin and Shafiro, and Galuzo, on the other hand, say that while there were a few individual cases of this happening, in general the manap class supported the Tsarist government. As is usually the case the truth seems to lie somewhere in between these two extreme positions. It must be said, however, that the evidence is more in favor of Shestakov and Miklashevsky than of Brainin, Shafiro, and Galuzo. The low number of native Kirghiz and Kazakh officials killed in comparison with the Russian and with the native Sart officials has already been noted in a previous chapter. In one of the official reports we find the statement, "in almost every volost the leaders of the revolt were the volost starshinas."[5] Very closely tied to this question of manap participation is the subject of *rod* ties. Here the evidence is that *rod* ties still had force. When the Kazakhs, both those who worked as hired hands and those who were self-employed, heard about the order for conscription of workers they immediately threw down their work and made for their own kinship group.[6] While the many changes that the Russians had brought in their train had done much to bring the disintegration of the old tribal order, in times of misfortune the latter still had force.

5. *Vosstanie 1916 g.v Kirgizstane*, p. 112.

6. Pamyatnaya zapiska o kirgizakh: "K istorii vosstaniya kirghiz v 1916 g.," op. cit., p. 63.

One point almost all of the Soviet writers mention—that the revolt was of great significance in preparing the people for their part in the Bolshevik Revolution soon to come. They readily admit that this was a nationalist-religious movement and not one of the proletariat pursuing class-conscious goals. Nevertheless this was a "progressive" movement in their view. In its progress it hastened the cleavage between the rich and the poor. It showed the latter the true nature of the wealthy class and of its adherence to the reactionary Tsarist government, especially among the Sarts. The revolt laid the groundwork for the participation of the poor in the Bolshevik Revolution on the side of the Communists. The revolt not only hastened the *morcellement* taking place between the wealthy and poor segments of society but the struggle against the Tsarist forces *per se* brought great profit to the poor in fitting them for their future role. In the words of Lenin, "The real education of the mass can never be separated from the independent political, and especially revolutionary, struggles of the same mass. Only battle instructs the exploited class, only battle discloses to it the measure of its strength, widens its horizon, raises its capabilities, clarifies its understanding, forges its will."[7]

B. The Recent Soviet Interpretation

All of the preceding Soviet authors deal with the Revolt of 1916 as furthering the Bolshevik cause. They view the revolt as but a logical outcome of the repressive, cruel policies of Tsarism and that hence the people of Turkistan did right to rebel when these policies became especially unbearable as they did become just before the revolt broke out. Moreover, as has been seen, such a revolt, despite its identification with remnants of the old feudal order and the Moslem clergy, was "progressive" in that it furthered the Marxian historical process by aligning the poor against the rich and striking the first blow against Tsarism prior to the February revolution. Such an interpretation of

7. N. Lenin, *Izbrannye proizvedeniya*, vol. II (1935 edition), p. 7, "Doklad o revolyutsii 1905 g."

the Revolt of 1916, the Andijan uprising, and struggles of native peoples against Tsarism in other parts of the Russian Empire, such as the struggle of Sheik Shamil in Dagestan from 1834 to 1859, fitted in well with the historical fashion among Soviet historians after the Bolshevik Revolution of painting Russia's past under the Tsars in the darkest hues. A sharp black-and-white contrast with Russia's new life under Communism was the order of the day among Soviet historians. This denigration of Russia's past was vigorously promoted by the eminent Marxist historian, M. N. Pokrovsky, who, through official favor, was able to enforce his views upon his colleagues and rule the Russian historical profession with an iron hand.[8] With Pokrovsky's death in 1932 the system of history that he had so carefully built up was at first slowly and then with a greatly stepped-up intensity subjected to criticism. In the end the views of Pokrovsky were officially condemned by the government and a totally different interpretation was given to many of the figures of and incidents of Tsarist times. Figures like Ivan the Terrible and Peter the Great were no longer to be looked upon as evil Tsars oppressing the Russian people but as great statesmen and historical figures. Minin and Pozharsky, who led the fight in 1612 against Polish intervention in Russia during the "Time of Troubles" now became great Russian patriots while the resistance to Napoleon's invasion in 1812, formerly viewed as purely an affair of the Tsarist government in which the people took no part, was now portrayed as a great and noble struggle upon the part of the Russian people against the hated foreign invader.

Part and parcel of this reinterpretation of Russian history was the new way of viewing the conquest and incorporation into the Russian Empire of such areas as the Ukraine, the Caucasus, and Central Asia. Whereas writers in the Pokrovsky era had shown a lively sympathy with any offering of resistance by the natives of these areas to the Tsar-

8. Many Soviet historians suffered from the sting of his pen and tongue. Thus his criticism led to the imprisonment and subsequent exile to Central Asia of Eugene Tarlé, now one of the most prominent Soviet historians. See A. Mazour, *Modern Russian Historiography* (Berkeley, 1939), p. 85.

ist government's encroachment and subjugation, Soviet writers, beginning in the late '30s, took a different tack with their "theory of the lesser evil" which they now evolved. Such non-Russian border areas as the three areas mentioned, so these historians now asserted, were fated to come under the rule either of Russia or of its other strong neighbors. Faced with this "either or" proposition it was to the advantage of these peoples to be incorporated into Russia rather than into the domains of their other neighbors as Russia was a "lesser evil." Russian imperialism, so these writers now asserted, dealt less harshly with the native peoples and brought more benefits and less oppression and exploitation than did the imperialism of other countries.[9] Thus it was a "lesser evil" for Georgia to become absorbed by Russia rather than by Turkey or Persia, who also had designs on this territory. Similarly, in the cause of the Ukraine, fated to become a part either of Poland or of Turkey or of Russia, the absorption by Russia was the least undesirable happening.

In recent years this theory of the "lesser evil" has been abandoned in favor of the interpretation that absorption by Tsarist Russia was a positive good for the native peoples bringing to them civilization and technical advancement. An article by the Tajik historian, B. Gafurov, is typical in this regard.[10] Gafurov states that "the joining to Russia of Central Asia and Kazakhstan had for them a great progressive significance." Union meant not only union with the Russia of the Romanovs but with the Russia of a host of great thinkers and artists, such as Lenin, Plekhanov, and Tschaikovsky. It brought contact not only with Russian civilization but with the ideas of Marxism-Leninism. Union meant the end of the old feudal patriarchal economy; the setting up of industrial enterprises and the expansion of internal and external trade followed in the wake of Russian arms. Union meant the end of the slave trade in Central Asia and the end of internecine strife. The final point made by Gafurov is that if Central Asia and Kazakhstan had

9. See "On the Question of the Lesser Evil Formula; Letter to the Editors from M. Nechkina" (in Russian), *Voprosi istorii*, no. 4 (1951), pp. 44–48.

10. B. Gafurov, "Towards a Marxist Elucidation of the History of the Tajik People and the History of Its Culture" (in Russian), *Kommunist Tadzhikistana*, July 26, 1951.

not been incorporated into Russia they would have become colonies of English imperialism and would have shared the same fate as the peoples of India.

A corollary of this new characterization of the Russian absorption of non-Russian peoples is the new way of interpreting national movements of these peoples under the Tsarist regime. Whereas in the Pokrovsky era these movements were usually characterized as being essentially "progressive" now some movements are praised as being "progressive" while others are condemned as being "reactionary." The Andijan uprising of 1898 and the Revolt of 1916 in its Turkoman phase fall into this latter category. "Lenin and Stalin declared," states one article dealing with the Andijan uprising, "that there are national movements that are progressive and liberating and those that are reactionary."[11] While the author does not go on to give any general rule as to how one may tell whether a particular national movement is "reactionary" or "progressive," it becomes abundantly clear from the reasoning used in classifying specific revolts as either reactionary or progressive in this and other articles what criteria are used. National movements that were directed not only against Russian Tsarist officials but the Russians *as such* (settlers, merchants, etc.) are condemned as being "reactionary" while those directed against the native "exploiter" class—the aristocracy, merchants, and landlords—and not at the Russians as such are termed "progressive" and of a genuine revolutionary nature. In giving examples of the latter type of national movement B. Gafurov declares: "Of a genuine revolutionary, national-liberating nature were many of the uprisings against the Emir of Bukhara after the revolution of 1905–1907 in the mountainous sections of the Kuljab, Boldjuan, and Kurgan-Tyubin bekdoms."[12]

Examples of "reactionary uprisings" are: the Revolt of 1916, in the area of Turkmenia and Tadjikistan, the Andijan uprising, and the uprising of the Kazakhs under Sultan Kenesary Kasymov (1837–1846). It

11. A. Khasanov, "K voprosu o kharaktere Andizhanskogo vosstaniya," *Sovetskaya Kirgiziya*, May 26, 1951.

12. Gafurov, op. cit.

is significant that these uprisings were directed against the Russians in the main and not primarily against the native officials.

As for the Revolt of 1916 itself the great attention recently among Soviet historians has been concentrated upon the Turkoman phase though it is safe to conjecture that the new interpretation of national uprising will be applied soon to the other phases of the revolt. Probably the most detailed elaboration thus far of the Turkoman phase is contained in an article in the September 1951 issue of *Voprosi istorii.*[13] According to the author of this article the following conclusions may be drawn from the facts of the Revolt of 1916 in Turkmenia:

1. The opposition in 1916 of part of the peasant masses of Turkmenia to Tsarist Russia cannot be called a national-liberation movement and, much less, a revolutionary movement.
2. The movement was organized and provoked by the Turkoman feudal-patriarchal and ecclesiastical aristocracy—a network of agents of Persia, Turkey, and Germany.
3. The demands which the feudal-patriarchal and ecclesiastical aristocracy put forward were reactionary: a return to the old feudal patriarchal institutions, expulsion of the Russians from Turkmenia, annexation to Persia and Afghanistan and later on to Turkey.
4. The bulk of the peasantry of Turkmenia did not participate in this movement. The tribes of Yomuds from regions bordering on Persia took part, in the main.
5. The method of fighting was not revolutionary (the burning of Russian settlements, attacks upon frontier posts, the blowing up of bridges, the dismantling of railway tracks, the destruction of telegraphic communications, and the murdering of railway workers and employees).

The author concludes by stating that the Revolt of 1916 in Turkmenia prevented the formation of a united fighting front between the Turkoman working class and the Russian working class, that the movement was anti-Russian, that the most backward Turkomans along the Persian frontier and headed by a feudal-patriarchal hierarchy

13. Yu Tarasov, "On the Character of the Movement of 1916 in Turkmenia," *Voprosi istorii*, no. 9 (1951), pp. 76–96.

took part. However, the most class-conscious part of these tribes did not participate, nor did the bulk of the Turkomans.

There is some evidence to show that the Revolt of 1916 may be found "progressive" by Soviet writers in the future in some of its other locales, the explanation being that the revolt there took on a very different turn than among the Turkomans. An extract from the article of B. Gafurov already cited gives hint of such a possibility:

> Many historians of the Central Asian republics, including Tadjikistan, affirmed categorically that the uprising of 1916 was national-liberating and progressive. Moreover, in their appraisal of the character of these uprisings many historians did not deduce this from the concrete conditions of each district of Central Asia. They did not consider the possibility that in some places the uprising broke out spontaneously and was directed not only against the Tsarist government but also against the local exploiters, while in other places they were utilized by reactionary feudal elements and fanatical clergy in their own interests.
>
> These elements made the attempt to direct the uprising against the Russians everywhere under the watchword of a holy war for the faith. There are individual instances of the participation of agents of Turkey in the uprising.[14]

Gafurov then admits that in his book *The History of the Tadjik People* he likewise did not distinguish among the circumstances under which uprising broke out in the various localities in Central Asia and, moreover, gave an erroneous interpretation of the revolt, stating that it prepared the masses of Central Asia for the October Revolution.

The mention of the participation of Turkish and other foreign agents in both the Revolt of 1916 and in the Andijan uprising by recent Soviet authors is also significant as earlier Soviet writers discounted or minimized foreign influence, participation, and aid.

C. In Summing Up

The passing of a half century of Russian rule in Turkistan still found the native population living a life which was, to use the words of Hobbes, "brutish, nasty, and short." The material condition of the

14. Gafurov, op. cit.

mass of the population had, if anything, grown worse, though the wealthy members of the native society undoubtedly benefited by the transition. Such marks of civilization as modern roads, hospitals, sanitation, etc. remained completely strange to the native peoples. Only the modern methods of exploitation disturbed the millennial torpor of the subject peoples, and only too often were only the seamy sides of Russian civilization to be noted among the natives who adopted Western life.

In truth the Russian was ill-fitted for the task of civilizing the Asian. Western culture was represented in Russia only too often by only a thin veneer of the upper classes. The remainder of the Russian population was on a cultural level which at best case was not too far above that existing among the native peoples of Asiatic Russia, while the glacial advance of Russia into Central Asia produced a commingling of peoples.[15] While the policy of Russia was directed in an increasing measure towards Asia, unlike England she effected no significant influence intellectually or culturally upon Asia. In the words of one authority, "The Russian Tsarist regime was itself far too Asiatic to be able to influence Asia."[16]

The policy of *laissez faire* in the cultural life of the native had proved a complete failure. The absence of control over the native religious schools preserved a hot-bed of propaganda against the Russian government. The failure to provide schools in which the natives might learn Russian preserved an obstacle preventing the latter from coming into closer contact with the Russians and from rising to superior posts in government and industry which the native legally could do. It is significant to note in this regard that one of the things the Kirghiz and Kazakhs complained about to Kuropatkin in his tour of the country was that the great sums levied on them for education were not used, that the schools that were furnished did not give their children a

15. On this see Owen Lattimore, "Inner Asian Frontiers. Chinese and Russian Margins of Expansion," *Journal of Economic History*, vol. VII, no. 1 (May 1947), p. 28.

16. Kohn, op. cit., p. 128.

knowledge of the Russian language.[17] While among the Sarts the mullahs strongly opposed lay schools, a determined program by the government would have probably been attended by success.

The system of local autonomy for the natives in government also proved a failure. Except among the Turkomans Kuropatkin found general dissatisfaction among the native people in regard to their native volost heads and kazii or judges. This system of democracy below and autocracy above broke down for a number of reasons. The Russian officials were altogether too few to supervise the system properly. Their bad material condition made them susceptible to bribes and corruption while the lack of an opportunity for a career produced an attitude of frustration. The barrier of language and of different cultures was not broken, owing to the lack of lay schools teaching Russian and the Russian way of life, to the Russian government's prohibition of any proselytizing activity by the Orthodox Church, and to a disinclination on the part of too many of the Russian officials to learn the native language. The old khanate official had been arbitrary, unjust, and corrupt but at least the population knew his ways as he was one of them; the official, on the other hand, knew the limit beyond which it was not wise to push his exactions, as the people might successfully revolt. The native official under Russian rule, however, had at his call the unlimited might of the Russian army in any case where the population might resist his demands. The language barrier prevented the natives from going over the heads of these officials to present their grievances to the Russians, while Russian laws were completely alien to them. The upshot of all this was that a wider gulf was created between the two peoples. As Kuropatkin was to note in his journal, "We have not moved closer but farther away from the native sedentary population in the last 30 years."[18] The seam across the fabric was clearly revealed in the cold, ineluctable fact of revolt. The native population vented its discontent and dislike in attacks upon

17. Journal of Kuropatkin, "Vosstanie 1916 g.v Srednei Azii," op. cit., p. 66.
18. Ibid., p. 64.

Russian railway workers, parties of statisticians and forest guards, and on the Russian population. The latter were equally savage in their reprisals.

Of decisive importance in limiting the scope of the revolt was the question of the timing of the various outbreaks among the Kirghiz and Kazakhs, Sarts, and Turkomans. As we have already seen, the revolt among the Kazakhs and Kirghiz did not begin until the Sart uprising had been put down, while the struggle among the Turkomans did not reach its full intensity until November, that is after the revolt in Semirechie had been suppressed for the most part. Thus Kuropatkin was able to shuttle troops, thanks to the railway, between the troubled areas without ever having to cope with a synchronous revolt in all the areas of Russian Central Asia and Kazakhstan. What would have happened in the latter event is of course speculation but it is perhaps not too extravagant to say that in such an event the Russian Revolution would have begun in Turkistan and not in Petrograd, and would have begun several months earlier than it did. Nothing succeeds like success, as the saying goes, and the success which would have attended such a combined effort would have induced many waverers to throw their lot in with the insurgents. In addition there is a possibility that outside help might have been forthcoming if the movement had seemed destined to succeed. Afghanistan, though neutral during the war, strongly favored the cause of the Central Powers and seemed on the point of joining them in the war. A revolt of dimensions larger than that which occurred in Central Asia might well have been enough to tip the balance in favor of war and intervention in Turkistan. In such an event the khanate of Bukhara might have been forced to join in the movement against the Russians, owing to its geographical position in between Afghanistan and the areas of the revolt.

The revolt revealed the complete antipathy between the nomads and the Sarts. The shows of resistance of each of these peoples took place in a vacuum with no coordination or cooperation between them. The ways of these two basic modes of living were too incompatible to be bridged even in time of disaster and tribulation.[19] An indication of this hostility is served by the case of the events in Przhevalsk uezd. Here many Uzbek merchants carried on their trade and represented a large element in the towns of the uezd. Not only did these people show no sympathy with the rebellion but in some cases even stood against the insurgents.

The absence of a powerful pen to stir the forces of national liberation is all too clearly seen if we make a comparison with the history of Central Europe. In Turkistan there was no František Palacky to write a *Geschichte von Böhmen* and reveal to the people its history where before there had only been vague legends, and thus to create a feeling of historic oneness and prepare the ground for insurgent nationalism. Nor was there a Johann Gottlieb Fichte to deliver any *Reden an die Deutsche Nation* and thus stir the people to rise from beneath the heel of the invader and oppressor and free itself.

The lack of leadership was likewise a serious deficiency. Not only was there no person who could secure support from all areas of the country and from all peoples, but there was no leader who commanded the allegiance of even one oblast or people. Some names, like Kanaat Abukin, stand out, but these leaders extended their influence over only rather limited areas. There was no one to personify the revolt as Madali had done in the revolt in Andijan in 1898. Turkistan would have to wait five years for its Enver Pasha and his dream of a vast Pan-Turanian Empire. By then the opportunity had passed. Everyone was sick of the fighting and bloodshed and wanted to settle down to a period of peace and recovery.

The Revolt of 1916 was brutally suppressed by the Russians, but the old grievances remained. Though Kuropatkin removed some of the more crying abuses the basic situation remained as before. These

19. For a detailed exposition of the centrifugal forces keeping apart these two ways of life, nomad and sedentary, see Owen Lattimore, *Inner Asian Frontiers of China* (New York, 1940), pp. 469–475, 491–506, 511–513; see also René Grousset, *L'Empire des Steppes: Attila, Gengis-Khan, Tamerlan* (Paris, 1948), pp. 495–496.

grievances were to exist into the Bolshevik Revolution and it was only after a long and hard fight, with much native bloodshed, that they were partially removed. The characteristics associated with the Revolt of 1916 were to reappear again and again. The Basmachi movement was to flare up anew while a new battle was to be fought under the leadership of Enver Pasha. The hatred between the Russian and the Moslem was to be flagrantly manifested after the overthrow of the Provisional Government when the local Bolsheviks allowed to the Moslems only two seats out of the seven on the Executive Committee despite the fact that they made up 95 percent of the population, while the Sovnarkom or Council of People's Commissars was made up entirely of Russians. When the natives convened assemblies to rectify this situation the Bolsheviks used this as a pretext for a savage repression of the native population, during which the city of Kokand was laid waste and thousands of natives slaughtered.[20] A special commission had to be dispatched from Moscow headed by Broido to ease the situation. Though the natives were given a little more in the way of equality a great deal more still remained to be accomplished. Nor were other grievances removed. The Soviets did not stop Russian immigration into Turkistan and the proportion of Russians in the country only increased. The plans to make cotton the dominant crop of the country received new impetus and the native was placed even more in dependence upon his food supply from the outside.[21]

These are but some of the tendencies which had underlain the Revolt of 1916 and which continued after its suppression. To show in detail how the revolt reacted upon future events would, however, require a separate enterprise in the gathering and analysis of materials.

20. Limitarus, "Turkestan since the Revolution," *Asiatic Review*, vol. XIX (Jan.–Oct. 1923), p. 604–605

21. For a detailed survey of the economic changes effected by the Russians, see the article by Paul Henze, "The Economic Development of Soviet Central Asia to the Eve of World War II: An Examination of Soviet Methods as Applied to a Semi-Colonial Area," *Journal of the Royal Central Asia Society*, vol. XXXVI (July–Oct. 1949), pp. 278–296; vol. XXXVII (Jan. 1950), pp. 28–44.

Bibliography

1. Official Reports and Documents

"Andizhanskoe vosstanie 1898 g." *Krasnyi Arkhiv* 1, no. 86 (1938), pp. 123–181.

Broido, G. I. "Materialy k istorii vosstaniya kirghiz v 1916 g." *Novy Vostok*, no. 6 (1924).

"Dzhizakskoe vosstanie v 1916 g." *Krasnyi Arkhiv* 5, no. 60 (1933), pp. 60–91.

Great Britain, Naval Staff, Naval Intelligence Division. *A Manual on the Turanians and Pan-Turanianism*, Appendix B: The Disturbances in Semirechie. From Official Data. Extract from *Semirechenskia Oblastnia Viedomosti*, nos. 200–215, pp. 229–234; Confiscation of Land in Turkestan, no. 185 of *Turkestanskia Viedomosti*.

"K istorii vosstaniya kirghiz v 1916 g." *Krasnyi Arkhiv* 3, no. 16 (1926), pp. 53–75.

Ryskulov, T. R. (Editor). *Vosstanie 1916 g.v Kirgizstane: Dokumenty i materialy sobrannye L. V. Lesnoi. Pod redaktsei i s predsloviem T. R. Ryskulov*. Moscow, 1937.

"Vosstanie 1916 g.v Srednei Azii." *Krasnyi Arkhiv* 3, no. 34 (1929), pp. 39–94.

2. Books and Articles

Anson, A. A. "Vosstanie kazakov." *Sibirskaya Sovetskaya Entsiklopedia*, vol. 1, cols. 530–532.

Aziatskaya Rossiya (published by the Colonization Department of the Ministry of Agriculture). 3 vols, and atlas. St. Petersburg, 1914.

Bailey, Lt. Col. F. M. *Mission to Tashkent*. London, 1946.

Barthold, V. V. *La découverte de l'Asie: Histoire de l'Orientalisme en Europe et en Russie*. Paris, 1947.

Brainin, S., and S. Shafiro. *Vosstanie kazakkov semirechya v 1916 godu*. Alma-Ata and Moscow, 1936.

Brun, Capt. A. H. *Troublous Times: Experiences in Bolshevik Russia and Turkistan*. London, 1931.

Chokaieff, Mustapha. "The Basmatchi Movement in Turkestan." *Asiatic Review*, vol. XXIV (April 1928), pp. 273–288.

Curtis, William L. *Turkestan, the Heart of Asia*. New York, 1911.

Curzon, George. *Russia in Central Asia and the Anglo-Russian Question*. London, 1899.

Czaplicka, M. A. *The Turks of Central Asia in History and at the Present Day, an Ethnological Enquiry into the Pan-Turanian Problem and Bibliographical Material Relating to the Early Turks and the Present Turks of Central Asia*. Oxford, 1918.

Dobb, Maurice. *Soviet Economic Development since 1917*. New York, 1948.

Dodwell, H. H. (Editor). *The Cambridge History of India*, vol. VI, *The Indian Empire, 1858–1918*. New York and Cambridge, England, 1932.

Dunsterville, Maj. Gen. L. C. *The Adventures of Dunsterforce*. London, 1920.

Encyclopaedia of Islam. Leyden and London: V. V. Barthold; "bai," vol. I, p. 587; "beg" vol. I, p. 688; "ishan," vol. II, p. 533.

Etherton, Lt. Col. P. T. "Central Asia: Its Rise as a Political and Economic Factor." *Journal of the Royal Central Asian Society*, vol. X (1923).
———. *In the Heart of Asia*. London, 1925.
Evkall, Robert B. *Cultural Relations on the Kansu-Tibetan Border*. Chicago, 1939.
Galuzo, P. G. *Turkestan-koloniya (ocberk Turkestana ot zavoevaniya russkimi do revolyutsii 1911 goda)*. Moscow, 1929.
Great Britain, Admiralty. *Handbook of Siberia and Arctic Russia*. London, 1918. Vol. I.
Great Britain, Naval Staff, Naval Intelligence Division. *A Manual on the Turanians and Pan-Turanism*. London, c. 1918.
Grousset, René. *L'Empire des Steppes: Attila, Gengis-Khan, Tamerlan*. Paris, 1948.
Hanotaux, Gabriel (Editor). *Histoire de la Nation Française* (tome VIII), *Histoire Militaire et Navale*, vol. II. Paris, 1927.
Henze, Paul B. "The Economic Development of Soviet Central Asia to the Eve of World War II. An Examination of Soviet Methods as Applied to a Semi-Colonial Area." *Journal of the Royal Central Asian Society*, vol. XXXVI (July–Oct. 1949), pp. 278–296; vol. XXXVII (January 1950), pp. 28–44.
Hudson, Alfred E. "Kazakh Social Structure." *Yale University Publications in Anthropology*, no. 20. New Haven, 1928.
Jochelson, Waldemar. *Peoples of Asiatic Russia*. New York, 1928.
Jorré, Georges. *The Soviet Union: The Land and Its People*. London and New York, 1950.
Kohn, Hans. *A History of Nationalism in the East*. New York, 1929.
Krist, Gustav. *Prisoner in the Forbidden Land*. London, 1938.
Kunitz, Joshua. *Dawn over Samarkand*. New York, 1935.
Lamont, Corliss. *The Peoples of the Soviet Union*. New York, 1946.
Lattimore, Owen. *Inner Asian Frontiers of China*. New York, 1940.
———. *High Tartary*. Boston, 1930.
———. *The Mongols of Manchuria*. New York, 1934.
———. *Pivot of Asia: Sinkiang and the Inner Asian Frontiers of China and Russia*. Boston, 1950.
———. "Inner Asian Frontiers: Chinese and Russian Margins of Expansion." *Journal of Economic History*, vol. VII, no. 1 (May 1947), pp. 24–52.
———. "Mongolia." *The China Year Book*, 1933.
Lee, Dwight E. "The Origins of Pan-Islamism." *American Historical Review* (1941), pp. 278–287.
Lenczowski, George. *Russia and the West in Iran, 1918–1948*. Ithaca, N.Y., 1949.
Lenin, L. *Izbrannye proizvedeniya*, vol. 2 (1935 edition).
Limitarus. "Turkestan since the Revolution." *Asiatic Review*, vol. XIX (Jan.–Oct. 1923), pp. 601–619.
Lyaschenko, Peter. *History of the National Economy of Russia to the 1917 Revolution*. New York, 1949.
Macartney, Sir George. Review of Mustapha Chokaieff's "Chez les Soviets en Asie Centrale." *Journal of the Central Asian Society*, vol. XVI (1929).
Mandel, William. *The Soviet Far East and Central Asia*. New York, 1944.
Masalsky, Prince V. *Turkestansky krai*. St. Petersburg, 1913.
Meakin, Annette. *In Russian Turkestan: A Garden of Asia and Its People*. London, 1915.

Miklashevsky, A. "Sozialnye dvizheniya 1916 g.v Turkestane." *Byloe*, no. 27–28 (1924), pp. 238–274.

Mindlin, Z. "Kirgizy i revolyutsia." *Novy Vostok*, vol. V (1924).

Nazaroff, Pavel S. *Hunted through Central Asia*. Edinburgh and London, 1932.

Pelliot, Paul. *Notes sur l'histoire de la Horde d'Or*. Paris, 1949.

Roustam-Bek, Boris L. T. "First Mohammedan Republic." *Asia*, May 1920, pp. 384–391.

Rozhkova, M. K. "Russkie fabrikanty i rynki srednego vostoka vo vtoroi chetverti XIX veka." *Istoricheskie zapiski*, no. 27 (1948), pp. 142–169.

Ryskulov, T. "Iz istorii borby za osvobozhdenie Vostoka (vosstanie kirghiz Turkestana protiv tsarisma v 1916 g.)." *Novy Vostok*, no. 6 (1924).

Sabit, Essad. "Die politische Lage in Russisch-Zentralasien." *Deutsche Rundschau*, Band CCII (1925), pp. 271–275.

Safarov, Georgii. *Kolonialnaya revolyutsia (opyt Turkestana)*. Moscow, 1921.

Salkov, V. P. *Andizhanskoe vosstanie 1898 g*. Kazan, 1901.

Schuyler, Eugene. *Turkistan*, 2 vols. New York, 1877.

Schwarz, Franz von. *Turkestan, die wiege der indogermanischen völker. Nach fünfzehnjährigem aufenthalt in Turkestan dargestellt von Franz v. Schwarz*. Freiburg im Breisgau, 1900.

Shestakov, A. V. "Vosstanie v Srednei Azii 1916 g." *Istorik Marksist*, no. 2 (1926), pp. 84–114.

Skrine, C. P. *Chinese Central Asia*. Boston and New York, 1926.

Skrine, F., and D. Ross. *Heart of Asia: A History of Russian Turkestan and the Central Asian Khanates from the Earliest Times*. London, 1899.

Stählin, Karl. *Russisch-Turkestan, Gestern und Heute*. Berlin, 1935.

Stepnyak, G. "Kirgizskoe vosstanie v Semipalatinskoe gubernii v 1916 godu." *Sibirskie ogni*, vol. I (1928).

Togan, Zeki Velidi. *The Turkistan of Today and Its Recent History*. Istanbul, 1940, and Cairo, 1947. In Turkish and Egyptian.

Toynbee, Arnold J. "Islam in Russia since the Revolution." *Journal of the Central Asian Society*, vol. V (1918), pp. 73–83.

Toynbee, A. J., and K. P. Kirkwood. *Turkey*. London, 1926.

Vaganov, O. A. "Zemelnaya politika tsarskogo pravitelstva v Kazakhstane." *Istoricheskie zapiski*, no. 31 (1950), pp. 61–87.

Woeikof, A. *Le Turkestan Russe*. Paris, 1914.

Young, George. "Pan-Islamism." *Encyclopedia of the Social Sciences*, vol. XI, pp. 542–544.

Zorin, A. "Kirgizskaya Sovetskaya Sotsialisticheskaya Respublika." *Bolshaya Sovetskaya Entsyklopediya*, vol. 32, cols. 362–382.

Index

Abdujabarov, Abdurakhman, 89
Abdu-Jalil, 54
Abdul Hamid, 7, 54–55, 60
Abukin, Kanaat, 69, 118, 140, 179
Abul-Khair, khan, 106
Adat. See Customary law
Administration of Turkistan, 37–46
Afanasev, Col., 88
Alash Orda, 100, 101
Alexeieff, Gen., 73, 93
Almasov, O., 103
Amlyak land, 15
Andijan uprising, 50–59, 60, 71–72, 144, 152, 171, 173, 175, 179
Anne, Empress, 12, 106
Azziz, Abdul, 55

Bairam-Ali, 35
Baitursunov, A., 64, 100
Barthold, 42
Basmachi movement, 124, 180
Begymbetov, N., 100
Bekovich-Cherkassky, Prince, 12
Beletsky, 28
Berg, Gen., 124
Bolsheviks, 63, 64, 168, 170, 180
Boxer Rebellion, 59
Brainin and Shafiro, 168–169
Broido, G. I., 63, 165–167, 180
Bukheikhanov, Alikhan, 43, 100, 103

Cadets, 64–65, 163
Chaev, 99
Chernyaev, Gen., 106–107, 123
Constitutional Democrats. *See* Cadets
Cotton Exchange, 22
Curzon, Lord, 8
Customary law, 15–16

Damskaya, Kresta, 69
Datkhi, Umarbek, 51
Dervish-khan, 49
Divedzhi, Shikhr-Khan, 140
Dulatov, M. J., 64, 103
Duma, 60, 64, 79, 163–164, 168
Dungans, 32–33
Dzainakov, I., 114

Efremov, 94
Elder Brethren Society. *See* Ko Lao Hui
Enver, Pasha, 147, 180
Erofeev, Gen., 74, 84, 93–94
Essen-Khan, 140
Etherton, Lt. Col. P. T., 146–147, 148–149

Folbaum, Gen., 29, 94, 107, 112, 115–116, 117–118, 122–123, 124–125, 131, 145
Forest Administration, 28–29, 31

Gafurov, B., 172–175
Galkin, Gen., 74, 94, 136
Galuzo, P., 143, 169
Gasprinsky, Ismail, 63
Geitsig, Lt. Col., 123
Geok-Tēpē, 7, 34
Gerrymandering, 46–47
Gippius, Gen., 75, 83–84, 94
Guidzhemal, khansha, 93
Grodekov, 42

International Geographic Conference, 8
Ishan, 50
Islam, 7–8, 47–48, 53–54, 65
Ivanov, Col., 90

Jadids, 61–63, 143
Jakambaev, Kasym, 120–121
Jihad, 49, 55, 70, 147
Jizak uprising, 86–93, 142, 153
Jui-ch'i, Ch'u, 130

Kalmyks, 12, 132
Kanitz, Count, 151
Kastalsky, Col., 160

Kasymov, Sultan Kenesary, 173
Kaufman, Gen. von, 17, 37, 123
Kazak, 65, 99–100, 114
Kazi-kalyan, 47
Kerensky, 79–80, 163
Khasanov, Karabek, 51
Khodoyarov, Mirza Yar, 88
Khoja, Nazir, 88–90, 92, 146
Kiakhta, Treaty of, 11
Knyazez, Jeksembek, 121
Ko Lao Hui, 145
Kolmakov, Gen., 75, 94
Kolpakovsky, Gen., 25
Kornilov, Gen., 69
Korolkov, Gen., 57–58, 122
Koryton, N., 21
Kulja, 33
Kuropatkin, Gen., 7, 46, 52, 57–58, 79–80, 86, 90, 93–94, 112–113, 122, 123, 124–125, 133, 138, 141, 151–155, 160, 176, 177–178, 179
Kushukbaev, Baizhazyk, 106
Kutebarov, Isetz, 13
Krivoshein, 19

Lenin, N., 170, 172
Likoshin, Gen., 75
Lu, 134

Macartney, Sir George, 134, 146
Madali, 50, 51, 53–55, 179
Madritov, Gen., 137–138, 151
Makkaveev, Lt. Col., 80–81
Martsohn, Gen. von, 77, 95
Ma-titai, 130
Matveev, Report of Lt., 162–163
Meyendorf, Baron, 42
Miklashevsky, A., 158, 169
Mogui, Bulgar, 115
Mulk land, 16

Nalivkin, 60
Narbut, Gen., 138
Nerchinsk, Treaty of, 128
Nicholai Nicholaievich, Grand Duke, 95
Nicholas II, Tsar, 52, 74

Okhrana, 61, 70–71, 72, 81, 143, 145, 154
Omarov, Okysh, 120
Orenburg, 17, 18
Orthodox Church, 58, 177

Palen, Senator Count, 19, 33–34, 59
Pan-Islamism, 9, 55, 56, 60, 61, 62, 64, 70, 72, 86, 143, 148
Pan-Turanianism, 9, 147, 179
Pan-Turkism, 9
Peter the Great, Tsar, 11–12
Pokotillo, Gen., 94
Pokrovsky, Gen., 124
Pokrovsky, M. N., 171, 173
Polivanov, Gen., 100
Povalo-Shveikovsky, Gen., 57
Prisoners of war, Entente Powers, 77, 150–151
"Pseudo-khans," 48–49

Ratzel, F., 9
Rawlinson, Sir Henry, 8
Reis, 47, 53
Resettlement Administration, 26–29
Revolution of 1905, 59–60
Rod, 42, 43, 140, 169
Romanov, Grand Duke Nicholas K., 87
Romanovsky, Gen., 123
Rukin, Col., 88, 90, 91
Ryskulov, T., 166–167

St. Petersburg, Treaty of, 33
Seleznev, 110
Shabdan brothers, 132, 140
Shamil, Sheikh, 171
Shariat, 15, 27, 52
Shcherbin expedition, 27
Shestakov, A. V., 84, 167–169
Shuvaev, Gen., 73, 94, 95
Skobelev, Gen., 57, 107
Sobolev, 90
Social Democrats, 60, 64–65
Social Revolutionaries, 60, 64–65
Sokolinsky, 125
Sokolovsky, Gen., 96, 102
Stalin, J. V., 173
Stefanovich, 131–132, 134
Stolypin, 19, 64
Stürmer, Prime Minister, 95
Sufism, 53
Sukhomlinov, Gen., 108, 109–110
Supreme command of June 25, 73
"Surplus" land, 27–28

Taranchi, 32–33
Tardzhiman, 63
Tashkent, 18
Tekke Turkomans, 69, 75, 93
Tevkelev, 163
Transcaspian railway, 17–18, 85, 149
Transsiberian railway, 26
Turadbekov, 89, 92
Turkistan-Siberian railway, 19
Tynyshpaev, M., 99, 114, 120

Ulema, 62–63
Ushzkuz, 65

Vakuf land, 16, 47, 53
Vambery, 47

Yunusov, Khusainbek, 114

Zotoglov, Capt., 88
Zyaket tax, 47, 53